# Adolf Hitler

**Holocaust Heroes
and Nazi Criminals**

# Adolf Hitler

## *Evil Mastermind of
the Holocaust*

**Linda Jacobs Altman**

**Enslow Publishers, Inc.**

| | |
|---|---|
| 40 Industrial Road | PO Box 38 |
| Box 398 | Aldershot |
| Berkeley Heights, NJ 07922 | Hants GU12 6BP |
| USA | UK |

http://www.enslow.com

*For Rich, who put up with my distraction and the all-nighters that disrupted our normal lives.*

**Library of Congress Cataloging-in-Publication Data:**

Altman, Linda Jacobs, 1943–
    Adolf Hitler : evil mastermind of the Holocaust / Linda Jacobs Altman.—1st ed.
        p. cm. — (Holocaust heroes and Nazi criminals)
    Includes bibliographical references and index.
    ISBN 0-7660-2533-0
    1. Hitler, Adolf, 1889–1945—Juvenile literature. 2. Heads of state—Germany—Biography—Juvenile literature. 3. Germany—History—1933–1945—Juvenile literature. 4. Holocaust, Jewish (1939–1945)—Juvenile literature. I. Title. II. Series.
    DD247.H5A8123 2005
    943.086′092—dc22

                                                    2004028115
Printed in the United States of America

10 9 8 7 6 5 4 3 2 1

**To Our Readers:** We have done our best to make sure all Internet addresses in this book were active and appropriate when we went to press. However, the author and the publisher have no control over and assume no liability for the material available on those Internet sites or on other Web sites they may link to. Any comments or suggestions can be sent by e-mail to comments@enslow.com or to the address on the back cover.

**Illustration Credits:** Courtesy of USHMM Photo Archives, pp. 41, 117, 140 (second from bottom), 141 (top), 143 (bottom); James Sanders, courtesy of the USHMM Photo Archives, p. 143 (top); Library of Congress, courtesy of USHMM Photo Archives, pp. 5, 7, 134, 140 (top), 145, 153, 155, 158; Lorenz Schmuhl, courtesy of the USHMM Photo Archives, pp. 140 (third from bottom), 142 (top); The Main Commission for the Persecution of the Crimes Against the Polish Nation, courtesy of USHMM Photo Archives, pp. 140 (second from top), 142 (bottom); National Archives and Records Administration, pp. 24, 27, 50, 62, 74, 81, 120, 127, 140 (third from top), 144; The National Museum of American Jewish History, courtesy of USHMM Photo Archives, pp. 140 (bottom), 141 (bottom); Reproduced from the Collections of the Library of Congress, pp. 8, 13, 38, 45, 65, 72, 88, 99, 106, 115, 138.

**Cover Illustration:** Reproduced from the Collections of the Library of Congress

# Contents

## Acknowledgments

*Special thanks to Alex Hollander, a Holocaust survivor and friend who shared his experiences with me; to Cynthia Parkwell and the Thursday People, who gave me a place to hang loose when I needed it, and to Beit Chavurah, for the chance to sing and to pray, and to forget for a time that people like Hitler ever existed.*

# Fast Facts About Adolf Hitler

**Born:** April 20, 1889, in Braunau, Austria.

**Parents:** Alois Hitler and Klara Pölzl Hitler.

**Education:** Dropped out of high school in 1905; Failed entrance exam for Academy of Fine Arts in September 1907.

**Work History:** Painted and sold postcards in Vienna, 1909–1913; Served in the Bavarian Army, 1914–1918; Investigated fringe groups for German Army in 1919.

**Political Career:** Joined German Workers' (Nazi) Party in 1919; Led Beer Hall Putsch in November 1923; Wrote *Mein Kampf* in Landsberg Prison from 1923 to 1924; ran for German president in 1932; Became Chancellor of Germany on January 30, 1933.

**Key Military Events:** Invaded Poland, launching WWII, on September 1, 1939; Invaded the Soviet Union on June 22, 1941; Defeated at Stalingrad on February 2, 1943.

**Last Acts:** Married Eva Braun on April 29, 1945; Wrote his last will and testament on April 29, 1945.

**Death:** Committed suicide in his Berlin bunker on April 30, 1945.

# A Youth in Austria

Shortly after noon on January 30, 1933, a man with strange, ice-blue eyes stood before German President Paul von Hindenburg. Other dignitaries in the room looked on as Von Hindenburg administered the oath that made Adolf Hitler chancellor of Germany.

Some Germans danced in the streets celebrating the victory of this man who had promised to bring a bright new day to their battered nation. Others hid behind locked doors, dreading the future under this man who glorified violence and talked about building a German "master race."

That night, thousands of uniformed marchers staged a torchlight parade through downtown Berlin. President Hindenburg watched the parade from his office window. The marchers acknowledged him with respectful shouts as they passed.

Farther down the street, Adolf Hitler watched from another window. Wave after wave of marchers passed beneath him, each roaring louder than the one before. Hitler stood erect and unmoving, taking the salute as his due. The saga of his new German empire had begun.

## Considering Hitler: An Overview

Hitler's entire public career can be bracketed between the final days of two wars: World War I in 1918 and World War II in 1945. In that time, this son of an Austrian bureaucrat started as an unknown corporal in the German Army and became one of the most powerful dictators in human history.

In the social unrest and economic hardship that followed Germany's defeat in World War I, Hitler told the German people what they needed to hear: that they would rise from the rubble of a devastating war to build a Reich, or empire, that would last for a thousand years. With this message, Hitler schemed his way to power, plunging Germany and the world into a war that cost nearly 50 million lives worldwide.

Not all those lives ended in battle, bombing raids, or other military actions. At least 11 million of them ended in a cold-blooded mass murder that came to be known as the Holocaust. Under Hitler's orders, the Germans killed Poles, Russians, Gypsies, and especially Jews by the millions. In the name of "racial hygiene," they also killed handicapped infants, children, and adults; homosexuals; the mentally ill; and the mentally retarded—just about anybody deemed unworthy to live in Hitler's empire.

Those who remained—the ones considered to be worthy by Nazi standards—would become a "master race" of Germanic warriors: blond, blue-eyed men who had the strength to take what they wanted and the ruthlessness to keep it. They would spread over Europe and eventually the world, displacing, enslaving, or killing "inferior" peoples to gain *lebensraum* (living space) for themselves.

It was a plan, put forward by a man who transformed his private hatreds into public policy. All manner of scholars and experts have tried to understand Adolf Hitler. Questions about him tend to fall into three broad categories: What forces shaped him into the person he became? How did he manage to come to power? How did he transform a civilized nation into the totalitarian, racist state that produced the Holocaust?

Albert Speer, a top Nazi who once idolized Hitler, called him "one of those inexplicable historical phenomena which emerge at rare intervals among mankind."[1] Speer was not alone in setting the Führer, or supreme leader, apart from ordinary mortals. Hitler's followers regarded him almost as a demigod. Some of his opponents, and eventually his victims, tended to demonize him.

Actually, Adolf Hitler was neither demon nor angel. He was a human being; filled with rage and hatred, fascinated by death and destruction. He had one true talent; he could speak with passion and flair, convincing others to follow him blindly.

## Hitler's Parents

One of the chief mysteries of Adolf Hitler's personal life was the identity of his paternal grandfather. Hitler's father Alois was born to Maria Schicklgruber, an unmarried domestic servant who would not reveal the identity of her child's father.

The birth certificate listed the baby as Alois Schicklgruber, father unknown. When Alois was almost five years old, his mother married Johann Georg Heidler. Many have conjectured that Heidler was in fact the father of Maria's son, but the couple themselves never made this claim.

Five years after the marriage, Maria Heidler died and her husband abandoned young Alois. Alois grew up in the home of Johann Nepomuk Heidler, his stepfather's brother. He did not change his last name from Schicklgruber to Heidler until he was an adult. His uncle asked it as a condition of willing his property to Alois and made a sworn statement that his brother was indeed Alois's father. On the strength of that, the name of Johann Georg Heidler replaced "father unknown" on Alois's baptismal certificate. For no known reason, Alois's paperwork used the variant "Hitler" rather than Heidler.

The change of name did not stop the rumors and conjectures; if anything, it increased them. According to one rumor, Alois Hitler's biological father was a Jew, the nineteen-year-old son of a family named Frankenberger. As the story goes, Maria Schicklgruber worked as a domestic servant in the Frankenberger home. After her child was born, the family sent money for his care until he reached the age of fourteen.

These claims have never been proven. Nazi-hunter Simon Wiesenthal made an exhaustive search of genealogical records in the area. He found no mention of a family named Frankenberger, nor of the supposed payments to Maria Schicklgruber.[2]

In a sense, the truth or falsity of this story is less important than Hitler's beliefs about it. So long as he thought—or even feared—it was true, it affected his attitudes and behavior. This could partly account for the viciousness of his anti-Semitism, the obsession with "pure blood," and the secrecy about his background: "These people," he once said, "must not be allowed to find out who I am. They must not know where I come from or who my family is."[3]

The Schicklgruber-Hitler family mystery very nearly stopped Adolf's parents from getting married. The intended bride, Klara Pölzl, was the granddaughter of Johann Nepomuk Heidler, brother to Alois Hitler's legal father. Though technically cousins, Alois and Klara referred to one another as "uncle" and "niece." Under any circumstances, the relationship was close enough that the couple needed special permission from the Catholic Church in order to marry.

On January 7, 1885, Klara Pölzl became the third wife of Alois Hitler, a man some twenty-three years her senior. He expected her to keep house, care for his two children by a previous marriage, and generally defer to him in all things. This was the role of a wife in 1880s Austria, and Klara Hitler played it well.

She was a good stepmother to Alois's children, but her own children met with early tragedy. Her first son, Gustav, lived barely two and a half years, and her daughter, Ida, only fourteen months. Her third child, Otto, died within days of his birth.

## The Fourth Child

On April 20, 1889, Klara Hitler gave birth to her fourth child, Adolf. After all the death and heartbreak, she protected him fiercely. She never let him far from her, and she tended to his health with great care.

One thing Klara Hitler could not do for her son was to protect him from his father. Alois Hitler ruled the household and all who lived within it. He was harsh, demanding, and ill-tempered. He punished every misdeed with a sound thrashing. He not only beat the children regularly, but he would also whip the family dog until it cringed and wet the floor.

Even when he was not angry or violent, Alois Hitler made the family home into a joyless, gloomy place. He demanded silence in his presence; the children were not to speak unless spoken to, and anything that might be considered back talk would draw an instant and harsh response. He would not allow the familiar *du* form of address normally used with family and close friends, insisting instead that the children address him formally, as *Herr Vater*, which means "Sir Father."[4]

**Hitler's mother, Klara, in a formal portrait**

In 1896, when Adolf Hitler was only seven years old, his fourteen-year-old half brother Alois, Jr. ran away from home to escape their abusive father. By the time Adolf was eleven, his six-year-old brother Edmund died of measles. As the only son remaining in the home, Adolf became the focus of his father's anger and ambition.

Alois Hitler was immensely proud of his status as a senior customs official. He considered himself living proof that a peasant boy with a grade-school education could succeed if he worked hard and applied himself. Civil service, he told Adolf, offered security, stability, and the opportunity for advancement. He could think of no better life for his son.

Adolf did not agree. As he would later say,

> Neither persuasion nor "serious" arguments made any impression on my resistance. I did not want to be a civil servant, no, and again no. All attempts on my father's part to inspire me with love or pleasure in this profession by stories from his own life accomplished the exact opposite. I yawned and grew sick to my stomach at the thought of sitting in an office, deprived of my liberty; ceasing to be master of my own time and being compelled to force the content of a whole life into blanks that had to be filled out.[5]

Paula Hitler, Adolf's younger sister, recalled that he "challenged my father to extreme harshness and . . . got his sound thrashing every day. [Adolf] was a scrubby little rogue, and all attempts of his father to thrash him for his rudeness and to cause him to love the profession of an official of the [government] were in vain."[6]

## School Days

Young Adolf Hitler wanted to be an artist; and not just an ordinary artist, but a great one, a famous one. His father would not hear of such a thing. Adolf would not enter a *Gymnasium*, or academic high school, where students studied art and literature. He would attend a *Realschule*, which offered a more technical and career-oriented curriculum.

On September 17, 1900, a disappointed Adolf Hitler reported to the Realschule in the nearby city of Linz. In elementary school, Adolf had been a good student and a playground leader. In high school, he was just a kid from the country, socially inept and rather odd.

One teacher remembered Adolf Hitler as

> a gaunt, pale-faced boy who was. . . . definitely gifted, but only in a one-sided way, for he was lacking in self-control, and to say the least he was regarded as argumentative, self-opinionated, willful, arrogant and bad tempered, and he was notoriously incapable of submitting to school discipline. . . . [He] demanded the unqualified subservience of his fellow-pupils, fancying himself in the role of a leader . . .[7]

On January 3, 1903, Alois Hitler died suddenly. Adolf mourned well enough and long enough to perform the duties of a son. Then he began pressuring his mother to let him quit the Realschule.

It took him two years to convince her because she believed that she should continue to honor her husband's wishes, even after his death. When Adolf was sixteen, she finally relented, partly because he was failing his classes and would likely be expelled anyway. It seemed best to let him pursue his future in his own way.

## The Lottery

Adolf wasted no time in adopting what he considered an artistic lifestyle. He spent his time in museums and libraries and frequented the Linz Opera House. There he met August

Kubizek, whom he called "Gustl," a budding musician who became the only real friend of his youth.

"Gustl" Kubizek soon learned the price of friendship with Adolf Hitler: Let him lead, never contradict him, and most of all, let him talk: ". . . our friendship endured largely for the reason that I was a patient listener. . . . He just had to talk and needed somebody who would listen to him. I was often startled when he would make a speech to me, accompanied by vivid gestures. . . . He was never worried by the fact that I was the sole audience."[8]

The young Hitler did not make small talk, had no sense of humor, and showed no interest in the opinions of others. He spoke out of a deep but unnamed longing to control his world and everything in it, to create a space where his fantasies seemed real and he was a person of importance.

Linz did not offer a big enough stage for such dreams. In the spring of 1906, Adolf convinced his mother to let him visit Vienna, the capital of Austria. In this old and near-legendary city, he spent two weeks seeing art museums, attending operas, and studying the architecture of its venerable and elegant public buildings.

He came home inspired, determined to live and work and think as an artist. Adolf's idea of the artistic life required more money than his family possessed, and he had no intention of getting a job. His solution to this problem was to buy a lottery ticket. He asked Gustl to split it with him—five crowns each to win a fortune.

In his book, *The Psychopathic God: Adolf Hitler*, historian Robert G. L. Waite pointed out that there was nothing unusual about a sixteen-year-old boy buying a lottery ticket and fantasizing about winning a fortune. However, Adolf Hitler took the fantasy to another level; he was absolutely sure that he would win. With the money as good as in his pocket, he made elaborate plans for spending it.

He and Gustl went apartment hunting. When they found a suitable flat, Adolf carefully planned the furnishings for every room. The apartment must be perfect, for he intended it to become a center of Linz cultural life. Musicians, poets, and artists would gather there, to listen enraptured as Gustl played his music and Adolf gave discourses on history, the arts, and many other subjects.

Adolf flew into a rage when his ticket failed to win. He railed against the bureaucrats who ran the lottery, the officials who ran the government, and anybody else who conspired to cheat him of his winnings.

## A Secret World

In Adolf's fantasy world, he was not only an artist-in-the-making, but a man of destiny. He envisioned himself as someone who stood apart from the common herd and could not be bound by ordinary rules. This vision shaped everything from his taste in music to his first love.

Adolf was twelve years old when he discovered the operas of Richard Wagner. He found in them a mythic world of pomp and splendor, with stories that praised the exploits of godlike heroes, yet often ended in death and destruction.

According to Gustl Kubizek, Wagner played an important role in Hitler's youth: "When he listened to Wagner's music, he was a changed man; his violence left him, he became quiet yielding and tractable. He no longer felt lonely and outlawed and misjudged by society. . . . [He] was transported into . . . that ideal world which was the . . . goal for all his endeavors."[9]

It was in the ideal world of his own fantasy that Adolf Hitler fell in love for the first time. Her name was Stefanie, and in Adolf's mind she was the ideal companion; sharing his interests, sympathizing with his goals, entirely devoted to his wants and needs. He kept this image of perfection alive by the simple tactic of refusing to meet the real Stefanie. He never even spoke to her on the street.

He did watch her, always stationing himself where he would not be observed. If he saw or heard anything about her that did not fit into his fantasies, his reaction could be very frightening.

Once, Stefanie appeared to be upset about something; she looked away and seemed to frown as she passed him. He took that as a sign that she no longer loved him, and he declared that his life was over. He would not only kill himself, he said, but Stefanie as well. In death they would seal their love for all time.

Adolf did not make good on these threats, nor did he ever speak to Stefanie. The closest he came to contact was writing an anonymous letter, proclaiming his love and asking her to wait until he finished his studies at the Vienna Academy of Fine Arts. Then, he assured her, he would return and they could be married.

## The Artist's Dream

In the spring of 1907, Adolf Hitler turned eighteen—an age when working-class young men were expected to take up a trade and become self-supporting adults. Hitler had never held a paying job of any kind, nor did he have any intentions of getting one. He wanted to follow his artistic dream to Vienna and its prestigious Academy of Fine Arts. He had to get there by September to take the academy entrance exam. The time limit weighed heavily upon him, and so did lack of funds. The previous winter, his mother had undergone surgery for breast cancer. Though she seemed to be on the mend, her medical bills had depleted the family nest egg.

Hitler might have missed the examination deadline if his Aunt Johanna had not stepped in to save the day. She loaned him enough money to pay tuition and support himself for a year.

So it was that Adolf Hitler arrived in Vienna in time for the entrance exam. The standards were rigorous; 113 candidates presented samples of their work to a selection committee. Hitler was one of eighty who passed this preliminary phase and was allowed to take the test.

After the exam, he was tired but supremely confident:

> I was so convinced that I would be successful that when I received my rejection, it struck me as a bolt from the blue. . . . When I presented myself to the rector, requesting an explanation for my non-acceptance . . . [he] assured me that the drawings I had submitted . . . showed my unfitness for painting, and that my ability . . . lay in the field of architecture.[10]

Hitler was still trying to absorb this blow when he got word from home: His mother was dying. He went back to Linz, apparently without telling anyone of his failure at the art academy.

Klara Hitler died on December 21, 1907. Shaken by her death and his own failure, Hitler remained in Linz until February. By the time he left, he had convinced Gustl to follow him back to Vienna. He envisioned the two of them leading a carefree and creative life as students in one of Europe's greatest capitals.

Like Hitler's other schemes, this one was partly fantasy and partly reality. The two friends did indeed rent lodgings in the city. Gustl did win acceptance into the Vienna Conservatoire of Music. Hitler, however, found himself at loose ends.

While Gustl studied, Hitler dabbled, creating one grandiose scheme after another. He painted pictures that would never be hailed as masterpieces, designed buildings that would never be built, and even tried to create an opera; a grand opus in the tradition of his idol, Richard Wagner.

After the term ended, Gustl went home to work in his father's upholstery shop, planning to come back to Vienna in the fall. Hitler remained in the city, imagining himself as a struggling artist while actually living an aimless existence.

In one last effort to salvage his dream, he reapplied to the Academy of Fine Arts. This time, he was not even allowed to take the test.

## Down-and-Out in Vienna

Reeling now from his failures and his losses, Hitler moved to smaller, shabbier lodgings on the other side of the city. He left no forwarding address, nor did he notify Gustl of his plans. That was the unceremonious end of a long-standing friendship.

He had spent all his money; only a tiny "orphan's pension" stood between him and poverty. Though the situation was near desperate, he still refused to get a job. In time, he ended up on the streets, getting food wherever he could find it, sleeping in doorways and on park benches.

Come winter, he took refuge in what today would be called a homeless shelter. There, a man named Reinhold Hanisch befriended the scruffy young vagrant. When he learned that Hitler had wanted to be an artist, he suggested that Hitler paint postcards to sell on the streets. To start this little business, Hitler swallowed his pride and wrote home for money. A few days later, he received a fifty-kronen banknote from his Aunt Johanna.

# August "Gustl" Kubizek

By day, August Kubizek worked in his father's upholstery shop; by night, he went to the Linz Opera House whenever he could scrape up the price of a standing-room ticket. It was there that this aspiring musician met Adolf Hitler.

Kubizek was more realistic about life than his friend. Though he dreamed of becoming a great musician, he did not consider ordinary work beneath him. He prepared for his examination at the Conservatoire of Music and, when he was accepted, became a diligent student.

On summer break, he went home to work in his father's shop. When he returned to Vienna, he found that Hitler was no longer there. Kubizek later wrote that he had "often racked my brains over why our long-standing friendship was so completely and suddenly broken off without any reason."[11]

Thirty years later, the two men met again in Vienna. The would-be artist had become chancellor of Germany; the Conservatoire graduate, a civil servant who pursued music only in his spare time. After that meeting, Kubizek became known as "the Führer's boyhood friend." He received so many questions about Hitler's youth that he organized his memories into a book: *The Young Hitler I Knew*.

That was enough to move to the Männerheim, a men's residence that charged a small rent and had much better facilities. Hitler painted the cards; Hanisch sold them on the streets. In time, Hanisch began getting assignments from frame makers, furniture upholsterers, and others who needed presentable if uninspired paintings for their displays.

The more work Hanisch was able to find, the less Hitler seemed able to do. He was chronically late in filling orders.

He much preferred jumping into one of the endless political discussions that took place in the Männerheim reading room. He turned conversations into monologues, ranting furiously against Communists, Socialists, bureaucrats, and anybody else he had decided to hate.

According to witnesses, he said very little about Jews. Reinhold Hanisch and others have claimed that Hitler was not an anti-Semite when he lived at the Männerheim.[12]

However, Hitler himself dates the beginning of his anti-Semitic "awakening" to that period. In a famous story from *Mein Kampf*, he tells of a brief encounter that aroused his interest in the so-called Jewish problem:

> Once, as I was strolling through the Inner City, I suddenly encountered an apparition in a black caftan and black hair locks. Is this a Jew? was my first thought. . . . the longer I stared at this foreign face, scrutinizing feature for feature, the more my first question assumed a new form: "Is this a German?"[13]

With his curiosity aroused, Hitler bought "the first anti-Semitic pamphlets of my life" and studied them. He began to see Vienna not as a center of art and culture, but as a city of Jews and other foreigners: "I was repelled by the conglomeration of races which [Vienna] showed me, repelled by this whole mixture of Czechs, Poles, Hungarians, Ruthenians, Serbs, and Croats, and everywhere . . . Jews and more Jews."[14]

Hitler grew to hate Vienna. He wanted to put it behind him and go to Germany. He got the opportunity to do that on his twenty-fourth birthday, when he received an inheritance that his father had placed in trust for him. As soon as he had the money in hand, he packed up his few belongings and headed for Munich. He carried with him his hatred, his rage, and a budding notion that he had a special "mission" in life.

# Molding an Identity

Hitler arrived in Munich at a time of cultural flowering, when a generation of young writers, poets, artists, and musicians experimented with new forms of expression. Hitler was contemptuous of all this innovation, keeping his distance from it.

He rented a room, bought some art supplies, and started doing in Munich what he had done in Vienna: producing watercolors of street scenes, which he sold in bars, cafes, and beer halls. He no longer called himself an artist but an "architectural painter," imagining the magnificent buildings he would create.

As before in Linz and Vienna, he did nothing to make his dreams into reality. He did not have the educational prerequisites to study architecture, nor did he try to get them. He drifted and dabbled, with no clear purpose in mind.

He called those early days in Munich:

> . . . the happiest and by far the most contented of my life.
> Even if my earnings were still extremely meager, I did

not live to be able to paint, but painted only to be able to secure my livelihood or rather to enable myself to go on studying. I possessed the conviction that I should someday, in spite of all obstacles, achieve the goal I had set myself. And this alone enabled me to bear all other petty cares of daily existence lightly and without anxiety.[1]

## Hitler the Soldier

When World War I began in August 1914, Hitler promptly enlisted in the Bavarian Army, having dodged compulsory service in his native Austria. As a German soldier, he was "overpowered by stormy enthusiasm" for the war.[2] By his own account, he fell to his knees and "thanked Heaven from an overflowing heart for granting me the good fortune of being permitted to live at this time."[3]

The "noble" and "heroic" struggle of Hitler's fantasies soon gave way to the bloody realities of trench warfare. He was assigned to Bavarian Infantry Regiment 16, commonly known as the "List Regiment" after its commanding officer. They went into their first battle near Ypres, Belgium, in late October 1914. Four days of fighting reduced a force of 3,600 men to only 611.

In the face of such staggering losses, Hitler reached a conclusion about the very nature of life: "It was with feelings of pure idealism that I set out for the front in 1914. Then I saw men falling around me in thousands. Thus I learnt that life is a cruel struggle, and has no other object but the preservation of the species. The individual can disappear, providing there are other men to replace him."[4]

This never-ending struggle ensured the survival of the fittest. This idea applied Charles Darwin's theory of biological evolution to social and political development as well.

In Darwin, the fittest organisms were not necessarily the strongest or most aggressive; they were simply the best-adapted to a particular environment. Hitler redefined Darwin's principle to conclude that only the strong had a right to survive.

## Finding Somewhere to Belong

Hitler honed his brutal world view on the battlefields of Europe. For most of his time at the front, he was attached to regimental headquarters as a dispatch runner. He carried orders and battle plans from headquarters to the troops in the field.

Though he never rose above the rank of corporal, he felt his job was important. The orders he carried set battles in motion and kept units in the field working together, even when they were separated by many miles.

Away from duty, Hitler kept his distance and made no close attachments. Many of his fellow soldiers regarded him as something of an oddball. He rarely smiled, let alone laughed, and frequently harangued his comrades about their lack of patriotism and devotion to duty.

Hitler's best friend at the front was a white terrier he named Fuchsl, "Little Fox." According to the story, Fuchsl scampered across the battlefield and into a German trench. There, the oddly serious young corporal found him. Fuchsl gave his new master what humans could not: unlimited love, unquestioning obedience, and a point of contact with his fellow soldiers. Hitler could not joke with his comrades-in-arms or discuss his inmost secrets, but he could talk about Fuchsl and show off his latest tricks. Fuchsl disappeared in August 1917, becoming one of Hitler's most enduring memories of the war.

The other memories were not so pleasant. Hitler was wounded in battle and later temporarily blinded in a

**Corporal Adolf Hitler (left front) with fellow soldiers in World War I. The dog is Hitler's beloved Fuchsl, who doubled as a company mascot.**

mustard-gas attack. Mustard gas produced symptoms that were painful, sometimes deadly, and always terrifying. A nurse who cared for dozens of gassing victims described "great [mustard-coloured] blisters . . . blind eyes . . . all sticky and stuck together . . . always fighting for breath, their voices a whisper, saying their throats are closing and they know they [will] choke."[5]

Hitler was in a military hospital when he got the news of Germany's surrender. The kaiser, or emperor, had abdicated his throne. Germany would become a republic and hope for mercy from its former enemies. This news was so shattering to Hitler that "everything went black before my eyes; I tottered and groped my way back to the dormitory, threw myself on my bunk, and dug my burning head into my blanket and pillow. Since the day when I stood at my mother's grave, I had not wept. . . . But now I could not help it."[6]

In time, Hitler's grief would turn into rage, and he would direct this anger toward two groups that he already hated: Jews and Marxists (communists). In time, he would connect the two, stating that communism was a Jewish invention. He may have based this on the fact that Karl Marx, whose ideas became the basis for the communist philosophy, was a German Jew by birth. It is also possible that Hitler lumped the two together because he considered both a threat to German nationalism and to the "purity" of German blood.

At the hospital, Hitler began pulling the ideas and experiences of a troubled lifetime into a "world view." In the rubble of a shattered Germany he believed he had finally found his life's calling: He would go into politics.

## Back to Munich

Hitler returned to Munich in November 1918, not sure how to begin a political career. He was not well educated; he had no political experience, no money, no influential friends. He convinced himself that these things did not matter; somehow, he would find a way to accomplish his goal.

In the meantime, he remained in the army, drawing an assignment that seemed tailor-made for him. He became a *vertrauensmann*, or *V-Mann*. This was an undercover agent that investigated extremist groups that might be a threat to the German government.

Postwar Germany was filled with such groups, and Munich seemed to have more than its fair share. They represented all points of the political spectrum, from a particularly intolerant form of German nationalism to socialism and communism.

In April 1919, communists seized power in Munich and terrorized the city. The national government sent bands of volunteer soldiers, known as Free Corps or Freebooters, to deal with the problem.

Hitler did not join the Free Corps in their fight against communism; instead, he continued his work as a V-Mann. He taught patriotism and nationalism to soldiers who were considered "politically unreliable." Some had been in communist prisoner-of-war camps, and the government feared they had been "infected" by communist teachings. Others were angry and bitter; German soldiers had fought and bled and died for a losing cause. Now the survivors came home to social upheaval and a shattered economy.

As a V-Mann, Hitler used his speaking ability to lift himself a notch above other instructors in the program.

## Hitler the Anti-Semite

According to Hitler's own statement, the anti-Semitism that was to mark both his public and private life began in Vienna but "matured" after World War I. His first known attempt to deal with Jewish issues came in a letter dated September 16,

1919. It came in reply to a letter from one Adolf Gemlich, requesting clarification on "the Jewish question" from the army information office.

> *Dear Herr Gemlich,*
>
> *The danger posed by Jewry . . . finds expression in the undeniable aversion of wide sections of our people. The cause of this aversion is not to be found in a clear recognition of the . . . pernicious effect of the Jews . . . upon our nation. Rather, it arises mostly from personal contact and from the . . . impression which the individual Jew leaves—almost always an unfavorable one. For this reason, antisemitism is too easily charac-terized as a mere emotional phenomenon. And yet this is incorrect. Antisemitism as a political movement . . . cannot be defined by [emotion] . . . but by recognition of the facts. The facts are these: First, Jewry is absolutely a race and not a religious association. . . . Through thousands of years of . . . inbreeding, Jews . . . have maintained their race and their peculiarities. . . . And thus [they are] a non-German, alien race which neither wishes nor is able to [change].*

Hitler went on to claim that Jews were "a racial tuberculosis of the nations," and to propose "systematic . . . elimination of the privileges of the Jews," with the "ultimate objective" being "the irrevocable removal of the Jews in general . . ."[7]

Many historians as well as other scholars agree that, at this point, "removal" referred to exile rather than genocide. The plan for systematic murder of the entire Jewish people did not appear until much later.

## The German Workers' Party

A few days after writing this letter, Hitler received a new assignment: investigating a group called the "German Workers' Party" for political reliability. He was not much impressed when he attended his first meeting. The group was small and poorly organized. It appealed mostly to working-class men who gathered in beer halls to bemoan the loss of the war, share their hatred of Jews, and discuss the failings of postwar society.

Though Hitler did not go to the meeting to take part in discussions, he could not remain silent when someone suggested that Bavaria should separate from the German Reich and become an independent nation-state, with Munich as its capital. Hitler launched into such a scathing attack on the speaker that the unfortunate man slipped out of the room.

Party founder Anton Drexler was deeply impressed by this fiery orator. Before Hitler left that night, Drexler pressed a pamphlet into his hands and asked him to read it. Hitler was duly impressed with the little book, seeing in Drexler's experiences a political development that paralleled his own.

About a week later, a postcard came from the German Workers' Party, announcing that he had been accepted for membership, and inviting him to a meeting of the leadership committee. Hitler wrote that he "was astonished at this way of 'winning' members and I didn't know whether to be angry or to laugh. I had no intention of joining a ready-made party, but wanted to found one of my own. What they asked of me was presumptuous and out of the question."[8]

There are different versions of how and why Hitler changed his mind. He says that curiosity got the better of him and he went to the meeting, then joined the party after much soul-searching. Another version of this story has Captain Karl

**31**

Mayr ordering Hitler to join the party to help spread its nationalist doctrine.

These differences seem entirely trivial, but they may well be early examples of the "Führer myth" at its beginning. Hitler liked to surround himself with mystery, to appear larger-than-life. He exaggerated his own role in important events and minimized the contributions of others; he injected fantasy and outright misinformation into statements about his early life.

Whatever the actual details, it is clear that Adolf Hitler joined the German Workers' Party in September 1919, intending to reshape it in his own image: "This absurd little organization with its few members seemed to me to possess the one advantage that it had not frozen into an 'organization,' but left the individual an opportunity for real personal activity," he wrote in *Mein Kampf.* "Here it was still possible to work, and the smaller the movement, the more readily it could be put into the proper form. Here the content, the goal, and the road could still be determined, which in the existing great parties was impossible from the outset."[9]

One of his first actions was to convince the leadership committee that they should hold larger, well-publicized meetings. This reversed what founder Anton Drexler and party chairman Karl Harrer had tried to do. They wanted to get more members so they could hold larger meetings. Hitler wanted to do the exact opposite: hold larger meetings so they could attract more members.

He bullied the others until they agreed to try his way. They rented a large hall and placed newspaper advertisements. About seventy people showed up. Hitler whipped them into a frenzy with an impassioned speech. For thirty minutes, he denounced those he hated and trumpeted the merits of an uncompromising German nationalism. His speech drew a noisy ovation and three hundred marks in contributions.

Meeting followed meeting, each better attended than the last. This man with poor social skills and few friends had an uncanny knack for arousing a crowd. He reduced complex issues to slogans, easily remembered and frequently repeated.

Hitler claimed that Germany lost the war because of a stab in the back, or betrayal, by communists, Jews, and the "November criminals" who signed the armistice of November 11, 1918. He tied this image of dark betrayal to the treaty signed at Versailles and the republican constitution created at Weimar.

The Treaty of Versailles forced Germany to accept full responsibility for starting the war, stripped it of territory, and saddled it with huge reparations, or war debts. The Weimar constitution replaced the familiar monarchy with a democratic republic.

Hitler's skill at exploiting these issues worried some party members. They distrusted Hitler's frenetic style and his way of taking over everything. If he was aware of these reactions, he chose to ignore them. He had joined the party to transform a small-time debating society into a real political force and he had no intention of letting criticism get in his way.

## Into the Political Arena

Anton Drexler boosted Hitler's ambitions by getting him appointed director of propaganda. Hitler soon went beyond the job description to draft a party platform, or statement of principles. Rather than present it to the committee, he went directly to Drexler, where he could expect a sympathetic reading.

The two men worked through the night, hammering out what would be known as the Twenty-Five Points. On his own,

Drexler would most likely have submitted it to the leadership committee for discussion and vote. Hitler had bigger ideas; he wanted to launch the platform at a mass meeting. They would hold it in the largest auditorium they could find and work for an audience of hundreds, even thousands.

Party chairman Karl Harrer openly opposed the idea. Even Anton Drexler had his doubts. Failure could destroy the platform, and even the party itself.

Hitler held firm; the platform was not only an ideological statement, but it also had tremendous propaganda value, and he meant to mine every bit of it. He pounded at the idea until the opposition finally gave way.

The meeting was set for February 24, 1920, at 7:30 P.M. By the time Hitler arrived at 7:15, two thousand people had crowded into the hall. Even those who came to heckle added to the impact of the presentation. Some got so caught up in Hitler's oratory that they stopped disrupting the meeting to hear what he had to say. So Hitler presented the platform and saw it affirmed by a cheering crowd.

As the party grew, Hitler decided it needed a different name, one that reflected its nationalist and anti-Semitic platform. In August 1920, the *German Worker's Party* became the *National Socialist German Workers' Party*, or Nazi.

Nationalism, as Hitler saw it, was not simply patriotic; it was *volkisch*. Literally, *volkisch* simply means "folkish," but its deeper meaning defies translation. *Volkisch* nationalism rested on the belief that a kind of mystical connection bound all Germans together and shaped their cultural, ethnic, and "racial" identity.

To spread the message, Hitler surrounded himself with well-connected men who could help him build the tiny party into a formidable force. For example, Captain Ernst Röhm had

# Anton Drexler

The man most responsible for bringing Adolf Hitler into what would become the Nazi party was Anton Drexler, a machinist by trade, a rabid nationalist by conviction. According to his own statement, he hated Jews and Communists because he felt that he had lost several jobs on their account.

Though uneducated and awkward, with little to recommend him as a leader, Drexler was a principal founder of the German Workers' Party. His booklet "My Political Awakening" served as an informal platform, applying volkisch concepts of nationalism, racism, and anti-Semitism to the needs of the German working class.

Little is known about Drexler's personal life. He had a wife, a child, and a home in a nice part of the city. Apparently, Adolf Hitler was a frequent visitor, especially during the time that he and Drexler were hammering out the party platform.

contacts with paramilitary groups as well as the Reichswehr (regular army). This stocky, battle-scarred bear of a man was a soldier's soldier, freely admitting that "war and unrest" appealed to him "more than the orderly life of your respectable burgher [townsman]."[10]

Hitler turned to other people for other purposes. Poet and writer Dietrich Eckart introduced him to wealthy patrons of the arts, who also happened to be nationalists and anti-Semites. Through Eckart, Hitler met self-taught economist Gottfried Feder and self-proclaimed philosopher Alfred Rosenberg. These three men helped to shape Hitler's thinking on anti-Semitism. In July 1920, Hitler met Rudolf Hess, the man who would become his closest confidante during the early years of the party. Hess idolized Hitler, seeing in him a nearly infallible leader who could lead Germany to greatness.

## The Big Gamble

Not everybody shared Hess's confidence in Hitler. Many had become nervous about his growing power within the movement. He was demanding and uncompromising, with little respect for the opinions of others. In spite of these flaws, nobody wanted to lose him. He was their biggest draw—the man everyone came to see and hear.

One thing Hitler's "star" status did not produce was a steady income. The party was always strapped for funds, and therefore unable to expand beyond the Munich area. Some leaders, including Anton Drexler, wanted to consider a merger with the *Deutschsozialistische Partei* (DSP), or German-Socialist Party, headquartered in Berlin.

The resulting combined group would provide the foundation for a nationwide movement. In late March 1921, Drexler negotiated a merger that would include moving the headquarters of the new party to Berlin. Hitler threw one of his temper tantrums, threatening to quit if the merger went through.

Three months later, another situation emerged to challenge Hitler's position. Dr. Otto Dickel from Augsburg made suggestions for improving the party and talked about an alliance of ultra-nationalist groups. Hitler yelled and threatened to quit the party. He then left the room.

On July 11, 1921, Adolf Hitler formally resigned from the Nazi party. Some members were glad to see him go; they were tired of his tantrums, his high-handed ways. The committee, however, could not ignore the hard fact that the party could not survive without its star performer.

To get Hitler back, they had to pay a hefty price. He insisted on being named chairman of the party, with dictatorial powers. There would be no more committee, no more voting, no more talk of mergers; Hitler's word would be law. Anton Drexler was furious at the terms, but he knew he could do nothing about them. Hitler took full control of the party and began to create the *Führerprinzip*, the leadership principle, that would shape its future.

# Growing Ambitions

Once in control of the party, Adolf Hitler began shaping it into his own image. He wanted to become an agitator, stirring up trouble to disrupt the existing social order and overthrow the despised "November criminals."

Hitler blamed them for all of Germany's troubles. They signed the armistice that acknowledged Germany's defeat in World War I. In hopes of getting better peace terms from their victorious enemies, they abolished the monarchy and established a democratic state. It became known as the Weimar Republic, after the city where its constitution was created.

Hitler wanted to destroy the Weimar government and remake Germany as a National Socialist state. He made no long-range plans for accomplishing this goal but clung to a belief that it had to happen. In his mind, the quest for power was not a matter of boring details and political compromises. It was larger than life, with an all-or-nothing commitment to total victory.

## Hitler the Agitator

At the beginning of his quest for power, Hitler envisioned himself as a revolutionary, fighting to overthrow the existing government. He recruited hardened street-fighters and former soldiers into what would become a private army, the *Sturmabteilung* ("storm troopers"), or SA for short.

These men terrorized party enemies and created disturbances all over Munich. Despite this, the authorities did not move against Hitler until one of his victims pressed charges.

The incident occurred on September 14, 1921, when Hitler decided to break up a speech given by Bavarian separatist Otto Ballerstedt, who was scheduled to speak in Munich. Because Hitler despised both the man and his message, he decided to break up the meeting.

Early in the evening, some of his men infiltrated the audience and found seats near the platform. As Ballerstedt prepared to begin his speech, Hitler strode into the room. This was the signal for the Nazis to swarm the platform, screaming Hitler's name and throwing the meeting into an uproar, which soon turned into an outright brawl. By the time the police arrived, Ballerstedt and one of his associates had been severely beaten.

Ballerstedt pressed charges, but not even that slowed Hitler down. While awaiting trial, Hitler continued disrupting rival meetings and instigating street violence at every possible opportunity. He assigned Ernst Röhm to build the SA into a formidable paramilitary force.

In January 1922, a Munich court found Hitler guilty of disturbing the peace in the Ballerstedt incident and sentenced him to three months in prison. He actually served only one month; the court suspended the other two.

The brief imprisonment did nothing to stop Hitler. He continued to agitate for revolt against the Weimar government and to surround himself with men who would share his vision and follow his orders. These early leaders of the party were a mixed lot, from shy, hero-worshiping Rudolf Hess to World War I flying ace Hermann Göring.

Hitler valued his followers according to their usefulness to him. So long as they delivered, he ignored their failings. In some instances, he even defended them against criticism.

## Spreading the Word

Along with developing the SA into a potent weapon, Hitler wanted to further expand the party's influence. On August 16, 1922, he spoke at a massive rally of Bavarian nationalist associations, while the SA made its debut as a paramilitary organization, marching under its own banners.

In October, Hitler made an even more dramatic appearance at a German Day celebration in the city of Coburg. The invitations had suggested bringing an escort to the proceedings. In his typical grandiose style, Hitler took full advantage of this suggestion: "As an 'escort' I appointed eight hundred men of the SA; we arranged to transport them . . . by special train. . . . It was the first time that such a special train was used in Germany . . ."

The organizers of the event met the train when it arrived in Coburg station. They brought a welcome, but they also brought a warning:

> . . . we were forbidden to enter the town with flags unfurled, or with music (we had taken along a forty-two-piece band of our own), or to march in a solid column.
> I at once flatly rejected these disgraceful conditions, [and] declared that the SA would immediately line up in

# Hermann Göring

Hermann Göring had an aristocratic background, good looks, and jovial manner. After winning acclaim as a flying ace in World War I, he presented himself to the world as a swashbuckling hero. Göring had no patience for reflection, self-analysis, or political philosophy. He wanted one thing from the party: power.

Hitler appointed Göring to high offices and showered him with honors and awards. In the days of struggle, Göring worked tirelessly to advance the party. His lack of ideology made him a realist who injected much-needed objectivity into policy decisions.

That changed after the party took control of the government. The struggle for power had made Göring bold and ruthless. The possession of power destroyed him.

He had no patience for routine administrative duties. Instead, he indulged himself in lavish living, "collected" art masterpieces by taking them from museums, and gorged himself on gourmet foods and fine wines. He developed a love for dressing up in outlandish uniforms, often changing costume four or five times a day.

The war crimes court at Nuremberg convicted Hermann Göring of crimes against humanity and sentenced him to death. Only hours before he was to be hanged, he committed suicide in his cell.

companies and march into the city with resounding music and flags flying. . . .

Coburg was a known stronghold of communist and socialist labor unions. The locals did not take well to this show of Nazi strength: "On the square in front of the railroad station we were received by a howling, shrieking mob numbering thousands . . ."

The infuriated workers first threw only insults at the marchers. When that did not provoke a reaction, they started throwing stones. This the SA men would not take; they plowed into the mob with sticks and truncheons. The melee lasted only about ten minutes. According to Hitler, when the battle ended "there was nothing red [no communists] to be seen in the streets."[1] Though that was an exaggeration, the story made excellent propaganda for the party.

## Foundations of the Führer Myth

About two weeks after Coburg, Italian dictator Benito Mussolini staged his famous March on Rome. Reports varied about what actually happened, but a debate about facts could not compete with the stirring legend of Mussolini leading some forty thousand ragtag Italian nationalists into the city, where they vanquished all opposition and installed a fascist government.

Fascism had much in common with National Socialism. Both systems were nationalistic and anti-communist dictatorships. Mussolini became *il duce*, "the leader," a near-mythic figure who embodied the fascist ideal of manhood and whose word was law.

Hitler aspired to the same status. The idea of becoming a living legend with godlike traits appealed to his vanity, his sense of "mission," and his growing belief that he was a man of destiny.

In creating his own legend, Hitler proved to be as good an actor as he was a propagandist. He cast himself in this larger-than-life heroic role and began arranging the details of his real life around the image of the infallible, all-wise leader.

Hitler knew that propaganda and role-playing alone would not secure his power. He needed an issue, an enemy, a great and heroic struggle that would propel him to national prominence. He found one in January 1923, when Germany defaulted on its reparation payments. Two days later, French and Belgian troops occupied the Ruhr region of western Germany, the most heavily industrialized part of the country. They meant to stay until Germany paid its debt.

Amid national outrage and fury, the Weimar government ordered a general strike of all German workers in the Ruhr. It asked the German people to put aside political differences and stand together in passive resistance to the foreign invaders. The government pointedly did not ask for violence or even hostile confrontations, only for a complete boycott on any form of cooperation with the occupying troops.

Hitler saw the boycott as a threat; anything that united Germany behind the Weimar government could be a disaster for the Nazi party—and also for the growing legend of the Führer himself.

## Days of "Destiny"

To prevent this, Hitler took the risky stand of refusing to support the boycott. All but ignoring the French invaders, he blamed Germany's plight on the November criminals whose treachery lost the war. They were ultimately responsible for the present situation, he claimed, and ordered his followers not to participate in resisting the occupation forces.

**43**

Had the boycott succeeded, it would have damaged Hitler's emerging status as preeminent leader of the nationalist cause. To his great joy, the government's strategy not only failed; it failed spectacularly, triggering one of the worst episodes of hyperinflation in history.

The government could not afford to pay the expenses of the strike and boycott, so it began printing more money. This weakened the currency on the world market. Before the beginning of the war in 1914, Deutschmarks had traded at 4.2 to the dollar. By November 1923, that number had soared to an unbelievable 4.2 million Marks to the dollar.[2] German money had become entirely worthless.

Economic chaos and social unrest brought demands for action; not against the French this time, but against the failed policies of the Weimar leadership. This presented a propaganda opportunity that Hitler could not resist. He knew that the Munich authorities had been fearing a Nazi *putsch*, or attempt to overthrow the government; he decided to give them one.

On November 7, he learned that the leaders of the Bavarian government would be speaking at a Munich beer hall on the following night. That was all the opening he needed.

With members of his inner circle beside him and a squad of SA men behind, Hitler marched into the beer hall, fired a shot into the ceiling, and proclaimed the revolution. SA commander Captain Hermann Göring positioned his men around the room, with instructions not to let anyone in or out.

Hitler himself held three top Bavarian leaders at gunpoint, demanding that they accompany him into a back room. Away from the crowd, he harangued the officials, alternating between extravagant promises and crude threats. At one point he brandished the gun and announced that he had a bullet

**Small meetings like this were normal in the early days of the Nazi party. Gregor Strasser sits at Hitler's right.**

for each of them and one for himself; that would be the price of failure.

When his prisoners did not cower, Hitler tried to impress them with the imagined glories of his new state. He said that the well-known war hero General Erich Ludendorff had agreed to head the army. Actually, the general had made no such promise.

Hitler's claim may have been an outright lie, or perhaps another instance of his fantasies spilling over into reality. Either way, he sent one of his men to get Ludendorff.

The general arrived in full uniform, obviously upset with Hitler's high-handed behavior. Despite this annoyance, Ludendorff's own fanatical nationalism got the better of him; he decided to throw in with the Nazis.

With Ludendorff's voice added to Hitler's, the three officials agreed to support the putsch and serve in the new provisional government that Hitler would establish. The men went out to the main hall to announce their decision to a wildly cheering crowd.

A beaming Adolf Hitler shook hands with three men he had held at gunpoint and one he had summoned with a lie. He thought that Bavaria would become a base for moving against his real target—the Weimar government in Berlin.

## The Unraveling

While Hitler's force handled the beer hall, other groups were securing important military and civilian targets. Wilhelm Frick and Ernst Pöhner led the takeover of the police station. Ernst Röhm and his men secured military headquarters. Other groups moved against various army barracks and Weimar government buildings.

After the first assaults, the revolutionaries did not know what to do. They held their positions and waited for orders that never came. Instead of taking overall command of the operation, Hitler went off to deal with a localized problem at one of the barracks.

During the time that he was gone, General Ludendorff allowed the three officials to leave, trusting their word as officers and gentlemen. That proved to be a mistake. The men immediately reneged on their promises to Hitler, claiming they had been forced to join him.

The putsch was falling apart, but Hitler could not bring himself to let go. Some kind of heroic gesture might at least salvage a propaganda victory out of the failed putsch. Hitler and Ludendorff discussed the possibilities and decided on a mass march, right into the heart of the city.

Some two thousand men formed up at the beer hall, many of them armed and looking for trouble. At around noon, Hitler led them out. Along the way, people gathered on the sidewalks to watch, some cheering the marchers on, some heckling them.

In the heart of the city, a line of police waited for the marchers, blocking their way. As the two groups faced off, a single shot turned a tense situation into a deadly one. In a brief but fierce gun battle, fourteen putschists and four policemen were killed, with many more injured.

Hitler himself suffered a dislocated shoulder. He ran from the scene, leaving his men to their own devices as he sought refuge at the home of supporter Ernst Hanfstaengl. The police arrested him there on November 11.

This seemed to be the end of Adolf Hitler's public career. Few would have believed that any political movement could survive a failed putsch, a jailed leader, and a floundering party. The naysayers, however, did not count on Adolf Hitler's skills as a propagandist and orator.

## The Man in the Fortress

Hitler made masterful use of those skills during his trial. He managed to turn the courtroom into a forum for his ideas. At times, the trial looked more like an enthusiastic political rally than a court proceeding. Though he could not talk his way out of a conviction, he did receive a light sentence: five years in Landsberg Fortress, a castle that had been made over into a prison. He shared a large and pleasant room with Rudolf Hess, and he was even allowed to keep his dog with him.

During his time at Landsberg, Hitler wrote *Mein Kampf* (in English, *My Struggle*), the book that would become the "scripture" of his followers in the Nazi movement. In its pages he clarified his grim world view. For example, he decided once and for all that Marxism (communism) was a Jewish invention.

He tied the struggle with "Marxist traitors" to the idea of lebensraum, or "living space." The Aryan race, as Hitler called northern Europeans, would expand eastward into Russia, destroying or enslaving "lesser" peoples along the way. Those goals did not yet include genocide, the systematic killing of an entire people. However, *Mein Kampf* reflected Hitler's ever-growing obsession with Jewish "evil" and foreshadowed what came to be called the "Final Solution" to the "Jewish Question."

> If at the beginning of the War and during the War twelve or fifteen thousand of these Hebrew corrupters of the people had been held under poison gas, as happened to hundreds of thousands of our very best German workers in the field, the sacrifice of millions at the front would not have been in vain. On the contrary: twelve thousand scoundrels eliminated in time might have saved the lives of a million real Germans . . . [3]

Hitler was not predicting the gas chambers of the Holocaust. He was remembering the gas weapons of the war and looking beyond them to contemplate deliberate mass murder. At that time, few people would have taken his statements as serious threats. Some, however, realized that Hitler's deep and abiding hatreds, combined with his peculiar ability to sway the masses, could indeed be a danger in the future.

On this basis, Deputy Police President Friedrich Tanner opposed requests for Hitler's early parole: "Hitler's influence on all those of a *völkisch* mind—he is today more than ever the soul of the whole movement—will not only stop the [decline] of the *völkisch* movement, but will unite the currently fragmented parts and lead great masses of those supporters . . . back to the [Nazi party]."[4]

The court did not agree; thinking that the party was dead and Hitler harmless without it, they granted his parole. On December 20, 1924, Adolf Hitler walked out of Landsberg Fortress and back to his old life. He would soon prove that the Bavarian authorities should have listened to Friedrich Tanner.

# 4

# A National Stage

Hitler's first order of business after parole was rebuilding the movement. It would not be an easy task; while he was in prison, the Bavarian government had systematically dismantled both the SA and the Nazi party. Nazis could not hold public meetings, wear uniforms, or publish the party newspaper. To further complicate the situation, internal rivalries within the party itself had shredded what was left of the movement.

With unusual restraint, Hitler did not plunge headlong into the tense situation. He went into near seclusion, preparing himself for a return to public life. He had decided one thing in prison: There would be no more revolutions. He would achieve power lawfully.

> When I resume active work it will be necessary to pursue a new policy. Instead of working to achieve power by an armed coup we shall have to hold our noses and enter the Reichstag against the Catholic and Marxist deputies.

> If outvoting them takes longer than outshooting them, at least the results will be guaranteed by their own Constitution! Any lawful process is slow. But sooner or later we shall have a majority—and after that Germany.[1]

Hitler was probably aware that some of his more militant followers would not be pleased with this decision. He relied on his ability to persuade them that operating within the law was ultimately the wisest course. The government would have no reason to interfere and political enemies no basis for challenging duly-elected representatives.

## Going Public

Before Hitler could hope to revive the party, he had to get the government ban lifted. Instead of going through channels, he went straight to the top. In a half-hour conference, Hitler convinced Heinrich Held, minister president of Bavaria, that the party was no longer a threat to law and order.

The government lifted the ban on February 16. Soon the party newspaper began publishing again. Hitler wrote a long editorial for the first issue, calling for unity in the struggle against Jewish Marxism. He even indicated a willingness to compromise for the sake of that unity.

The editorial laid the groundwork for Hitler's return to the speaker's podium on February 27, 1925. He purposely chose the same beer hall where he had launched the putsch. It was packed to overflowing long before Hitler made his entrance.

His goal that night was to assert his claim to unconditional control of a reunited party. He hinted at the possibility of compromise among the various factions, then made it clear that he would not allow anything to interfere with his leadership:

> If anyone comes and tries to make conditions to me then I say to him: friend, wait and see what conditions I have to make to you. . . . After a year you shall judge,

**51**

my party comrades; if I have not acted correctly, then I shall place my office in your hands again. But until that moment this is the rule: I lead the movement alone, and no one shall set me conditions so long as I personally bear the responsibility. And I once more bear entire responsibility for everything that happens in the movement.[2]

Hitler spoke for two hours, bringing the crowd to its feet in a thunderous ovation. In that two hours, he reasserted his authority and brought about an impressive display of party unity. For the Nazi faithful, this was inspiring. For the Bavarian government, it was frightening. They realized that Adolf Hitler's talent for rabble-rousing might well revive the party and make it into a bigger threat than before.

To forestall a Nazi renewal, the government banned Hitler from speaking at mass meetings. Similar bans followed in other states, crippling Hitler's public career. He was forced to leave the mass audiences to others and work behind the scenes, meeting with key individuals and small groups to reorganize the party structure.

## Difficult Allies

Hitler's forced retirement from speaking opened the door for other Nazi leaders to take a more active role. Some of them had an independent streak that worried Hitler. He was especially concerned about two men: his old friend Ernst Röhm and Gregor Strasser, a recruiter and party organizer in northern Germany.

Though Röhm was a loyal comrade to Hitler, he had ideas of his own about the role of the military in the Nazi Reich. When the SA was banned after the putsch, Röhm created a new paramilitary organization called the Frontbann. It gave dispossessed soldiers an army to join, a cause to support, and the promise of battles to fight. With this force at his back, Röhm would lead a revolution against the hated Weimar Republic and install a National Socialist government in its place.

Hitler wanted nothing to do with paramilitary forces or revolutions. Having decided to work within existing law, he no longer planned to overthrow the government. Therefore, he did not need an army. He needed shock troops—street rowdies in uniform, who could keep order at meetings, intimidate opponents, and even crack heads when need be.

When the ban was lifted on the SA, Hitler wanted to build an entirely new organization. It would not be an independent entity, but a division of the party, more a glorified police force than an army.

Röhm could not tolerate this. Though he remained loyal to Hitler, he could not function within such a structure. He therefore resigned his party offices, left the Frontbann to fend for itself, and went to Bolivia in South America to take a job as a military instructor.

Gregor Strasser and his brother Otto presented a different kind of problem for Hitler. Under their influence, the northern party had developed differently from the south. The Strassers took the *socialism* in National Socialism quite seriously. They believed that the state should administer the economy for the good of the entire population and provide social services such as medical care, education, and retirement benefits to everyone. In September 1925, Gregor Strasser called a meeting of party leaders in the area. They agreed to form a "Working Community" for the district. Party headquarters in Munich paid little attention until Gregor Strasser and his young colleague Joseph Goebbels decided to reshape the Hitler-Drexler party platform of 1920.

# Otto Strasser

Otto Strasser joined the Nazi party in 1925, attracted by its blend of socialism, nationalism, and anti-Semitism. He helped older brother Gregor to develop the northern wing of the party, based in Berlin. With Hitler working in Munich, the Strassers operated outside his direct control.

They created a socialist program that supported trade unionism, public ownership of key industries, and unemployment insurance, education, and medical care for everyone. The chief characteristic that marked Strasser's system as a nationalist version of socialism was its anti-Semitism and racism. "Everyone" meant Germans of pure Aryan descent, not Jews or other "inferior" peoples.

Otto Strasser's political beliefs became a problem for Hitler in 1926, when Strasser was made editor of the party newspaper in Berlin. He began publishing anticapitalist articles just when Hitler was trying to form alliances with wealthy businessmen. When Strasser refused to back down, Hitler expelled him from the party. Strasser created a rival organization called the Black Front. Though he attracted a small following, he could not match Hitler's popular appeal.

After Hitler became chancellor in 1933, Otto Strasser fled Germany in fear for his life. Brother Gregor, who had chosen not to quit the party, now chose not to flee Germany. Otto Strasser spent the war years in Canada.

Besides orienting it more toward the working class, they wanted to update it to reflect changed conditions and actual practices. When Hitler got word of this, he called a meeting of his own at Bramberg, on February 14, 1926. Strasser had already sent regional leaders a first draft of his proposed changes. Not only did Hitler forbid revisions, but he also insisted that Strasser collect all the copies he had distributed.

Like most things that displeased the Führer, Strasser's platform simply disappeared and the Working Community disbanded. Hitler wanted to make sure that such things would not happen again. At the annual members meeting on May 22, he issued a strong call for party unity, then formally declared the Twenty-Five-Points platform of 1920 to be unchangeable. It would stand for all time, regardless of inconsistencies or conflicts with actual practice.

Now the platform could not keep up with changing times or new ideas. This may have been what Hitler wanted it to be—a memento of a "glorious" past, in a party that was no longer shaped by platforms, creeds, or covenants, but by the singular will of the Führer.

## New People and New Directions

On July 3 and 4, the Nazis assembled in Weimar for the party rally. In view of the recent schisms, Hitler wanted to make the occasion into an impressive show of party unity. He also used it to introduce the new elite force that would one day terrorize Europe. The *Schutzstaffel* (SS), or Protection Squad, grew out of Hitler's personal bodyguard unit. He took advantage of the atmosphere at the rally to present the unit with the flag that went before the marchers in the putsch of 1923.

During this period of consolidation, Hitler managed to win Joseph Goebbels away from the Strassers. Small, dark, and clubfooted from a childhood battle with polio, Goebbels certainly did not embody the Aryan racial ideal. Still, he had an agile mind and a talent for speaking to the masses in terms they could understand. By recognizing his strengths and ignoring his shortcomings, Hitler won the young man's lifelong devotion.

Goebbels's diary during that period was filled with praise for Adolf Hitler. His entry for July 24, 1926, is typical of these frequent tributes:

> The chief talks about race questions. It is impossible to reproduce what he said. It must be experienced. He is a genius. The natural, creative instrument of a fate determined by God. I am deeply moved. He is like a child: kind, good, merciful. Like a cat: cunning, clever, agile. Like a lion: roaring and great and gigantic. A fellow, a man. He talks about the state. In the afternoon about winning over the state and the political revolution. Thoughts which I may well have had, but never yet put into words. After supper we go on sitting in the garden of the naval hostel, and he goes on for a long time preaching about the new state and how we are going to fight for it. It sounds like prophecy. Up in the skies a white cloud takes on the shape of the swastika. There is a blinking light that cannot be a star. A sign of fate?! We go back late! The lights of Salzburg shine in the distance. I am indeed happy. This life is worth living.[3]

Goebbels's enthusiasm notwithstanding, the period of the mid-twenties was quiet for the party. The mood in the nation had changed as the Weimar Republic hit its stride. The government had managed to stabilize the currency, get the economy back on track, and reduce unemployment. That did not bode well for political extremists like Hitler.

During this period, Hitler appeared in public less frequently than before. He devoted himself to party organization, preparing for the time when he could seek power within the framework of existing law. He concentrated on firming up his own position as absolute leader, building the SA into a formidable private army and transforming the party itself into a "shadow government." He created departments of defense and agriculture, and even a foreign department. He sent "observers" to represent him at diplomatic conferences.[4]

## Hitler and Mimi Reiter

The party so dominated Hitler's life that he did not seem to exist at all apart from it. He had no real friends, only associates; no interests or activities, no goals beyond raw political power. He was a talented speaker before large and faceless crowds, yet he had no idea how to carry on a social conversation.

He knew even less about romantic relationships. His involvements with women tended to be strange, like his youthful infatuation for Stefanie. He managed to build a whole love affair in his head without once speaking to her.

The most important relationships of Hitler's adult life occurred in the relatively quiet years between reunification of the party in 1926 and his emergence as a national political figure in 1929–1930. Without a crisis to galvanize him into action, Hitler hardly knew what to do with himself. He had no interest in the day-to-day routines of running an organization. He left those chores to underlings and turned his attention elsewhere.

While staying in the mountain village of Berchtesgaden in the early autumn of 1926, Hitler met Maria "Mimi" Reiter. He first saw her when both were walking their dogs; a slim, blond girl with haunting, pale-blue eyes.

He was thirty-seven years old at the time; she was just sixteen. He later discovered what he took to be a significant connection between the two of them: Mimi Reiter was born on an anniversary of his mother's death.[5]

**57**

According to Reiter's later account of their relationship, the future Führer of Germany behaved rather like a love-struck adolescent. He could not work up the courage to ask her out, so he sent one of his staff with a formal invitation to join him for a walk. She refused, but later accepted an invitation to hear him speak in the meeting room of a local hotel.

He called her by childlike pet names, kissed her passionately at unexpected moments, and sulked if she did not respond exactly as he wished on every occasion. Once, when he tried to kiss her goodnight and she turned away, he stopped cold for a moment, then came to attention, raised his arm in the Nazi salute, and shouted "Heil, Hitler."

In an equally strange, and far more cruel, episode, Hitler severely beat his dog, apparently to show off his "mastery" to Mimi: "He whipped his dog like a madman . . . with his riding whip as he held him tight on the leash," she recalled. "He became tremendously excited. . . . I could not have believed that this man would beat an animal so ruthlessly—an animal about which he had said a moment previously that he could not live without."[6]

When a shocked Mimi asked why he had been so brutal, Hitler told her that he had to punish the dog because it had "guilty feelings." With his tendency to be both childish and vicious, Hitler apparently never had a loving relationship with a woman of his own age. He attracted older women who wanted to "mother" him, and young girls like Mimi who were inexperienced enough to get caught up in his strangeness.

The relationship with Mimi ended abruptly in 1928, apparently because the Führer's involvement with a teenage girl had become a political embarrassment. They corresponded for a time after he went back to Munich. Reiter saved his letters and allowed them to be authenticated by an expert after the war. They were formal in tone and strangely impersonal, revealing almost nothing of Hitler's feelings or private activities.

## Hitler's "Greatest Love"

While Hitler liked Mimi Reiter, he was willing enough to give her up when the relationship became a liability to his career. The situation was different in 1929, when his niece, Angela "Geli" Raubal, came into his life. Daughter of his half sister Angela, Geli moved in when her widowed mother came to keep house for Hitler.

Like Mimi, Geli was still a teenager when she caught Hitler's eye. From the beginning, his attraction to her seemed to go beyond love. It became an obsession—a fixed and irresistible preoccupation with an idea or feeling.

Hitler watched Geli constantly, wanting to know every move she made. He would not allow her to socialize with people her own age, make her own decisions, control her own time. He hovered over her, apparently unaware that she chafed against his constant attention.

According to the household staff and others who observed the relationship, Geli tried to assert herself and break free of her uncle's hold. On September 18, 1931, she gave up the struggle. When Hitler stormed out of the house after an argument, Geli shot herself near the heart and bled to death on the floor of her room.

Hitler was devastated. Photographer Heinrich Hoffmann, who was one of the few to consider himself a friend to the Führer, described Hitler's behavior after Geli's burial:

> In my own room I stood in the window, listening to the dull rhythmic sound of the pacing feet over my head. Hour after hour, ceaselessly and without pause it continued. Night came, and I still could hear him,

pacing, up and down, up and down. . . . hour after endless hour, throughout the long night." He spent another day pacing and then drove all night until he arrived at the Vienna Central Cemetery where he stayed thirty minutes alone by the grave.[7]

Geli's death changed Hitler's life. Only days afterward, he set aside a piece of ham on his breakfast plate: "It is like eating a corpse," he said, and never touched meat again.[8] He turned Geli's room into a shrine, locking the door and insisting that nothing be changed. The only person allowed into the room was a servant, who brought fresh chrysanthemums every morning.

According to some insiders, the impact of Geli's death reached beyond Hitler's private life to his public one. He had always been eccentric, spinning grandiose schemes about racial purity, the glories of war, and the grandeur of an empire that would last a thousand years.

Ernst Hanfstaengl, the friend and follower who sheltered Hitler after the Beer Hall Putsch, was

> sure that the death of Geli Raubal marked a turning-point in the development of Hitler's character. This relationship . . . had provided him for the first and only time in his life with a release [of] his nervous energy which only too soon was to find its final expression in ruthlessness and savagery. His [relationship with] Geli . . . might in due course . . . have made a normal man out of him. With her death the way was clear for his final development into a demon . . . [9]

Despite his involvement with Geli, Hitler had paid attention to Eva Braun, a seventeen-year-old shop assistant at Heinrich Hoffmann's photography studio. After Geli's death, he began seeing more of Eva. She was a pretty blonde with the distinctive blue eyes of Hitler's mother.

He found her captivating; she did not quite know what to make of him. She described him to her sister as an "elderly gentleman" with "a funny moustache, a light-colored English-style overcoat and a big felt hat in his hand."[10]

Eva Braun did not know who he was; Hoffmann had introduced him as "Herr Wolf." She did know—or thought she knew— what he had on his mind: "The elderly gentleman was paying me compliments. We talked about music and a play at the Staatstheater, as I remember, with him devouring me with his eyes all the time. . . . I refused his offer of a lift in his Mercedes. Just think what Papa's reaction would have been!"[11]

Only later did Eva learn that the "elderly gentleman" was in fact Adolf Hitler, leader of the Nazi party. He began dropping by the studio, laden with flowers and candy for "my lovely siren from Hoffmann's."[12] Before long, he had become a suitor in Eva Braun's eyes.

## Adolf Hitler and "Black Thursday"

While Hitler was attending to his private life, the world economy plunged into what became known as the Great Depression. It started on October 24, 1929, which will forever be remembered as "Black Thursday"—the day that the high-flying American stock market crashed. This affected the economy around the world.

As unemployment soared and companies went out of business by the dozens, the Weimar government tottered on the edge of disaster.[13] It was just the kind of issue Hitler needed, and at exactly the right time; he had found a "sponsor" who gave him financial support and a national forum for his ideas.

Multimillionaire Alfred Hugenberg, a staunch right-winger and cofounder of the German National Party, owned a string

of newspapers along with Germany's largest film company. Hugenberg was a model capitalist, a wealthy business owner who created a fortune through investing capital (money) and employing workers to produce profits.

Hugenberg had money, he had contacts, and he had a cause: opposition to the Young Plan. This plan was an American scheme to reduce reparation payments by stretching them out over fifty-nine years.

Hugenberg recruited Hitler because he needed someone who knew how to reach the masses—and no one seemed better qualified for that than Adolf Hitler. With what historian Joachim Fest calls "shortsighted arrogance," Hugenberg thought he could use Hitler as a rabble-rouser, while keeping the real power for himself. He was neither the first nor the last to make that mistake.[14]

Hugenberg's group proposed a "Law against the Enslavement of the German People," which would have put an end to the Young Plan. In a special election, the voters overwhelmingly defeated the proposal, and thus the Young Plan took effect. It was a terrible defeat for Hugenberg, but not for Hitler. Free publicity in the Hugenberg newspapers had made his name known all over Germany. Hugenberg had served his purpose, so Hitler quietly withdrew from his group.

Though the alliance had benefited Hitler, it left him with fences to mend within his own party. The socialist wing criticized his alliance with Hugenberg and big business. With

Massive rallies allowed Hitler to whip up enthusiasm for the cause. Here, he strikes a characteristic pose, standing head and shoulders above the crowd. Hermann Göring stands directly in front of him.

the Depression deepening all over Germany, they wanted to organize the working class, not rub elbows with capitalists.

Hitler, for his part, stood ready to put politics over principle whenever it suited him. The Great Depression had given him an issue, while Hugenberg gave him money and national exposure. He had no intention of letting anyone or anything spoil such an opportunity.

**5**

# Chancellor Hitler

Adolf Hitler's enemies had as much to do with his move into the mainstream of German politics as did his friends. While supporters all but worshiped him, opponents made the deadly mistake of underestimating him. In this odd little man they saw only a talented speaker and propagandist; he had neither the background nor the training for politics.

Opponents failed to realize that Hitler was a crafty manipulator, with no scruples to restrain him. He could betray an ally, break a treaty, lie to friend and foe alike. He kept his closest associates off balance by giving them vague directions and overlapping responsibilities, while demanding their complete and undivided loyalty. So long as nothing was quite what it seemed, he could stand safely above the fray while underlings quarreled amongst themselves.

He was equally skilled in manipulating crowds, even "respectable" middle-class ones. He sensed what they wanted to hear, what they needed to hear. During the Great

Depression, he stressed lebensraum—living space—and economic reform rather than the "Jewish Question." He spoke tirelessly around the country, promising a nation stunned by the Great Depression that his party could save the economy and restore prosperity.

Hitler's campaign worked. In the election of September 14, 1930, the Nazis became the second-largest party in the Reichstag, or parliament, with 107 representatives.

## The Workings of the Reichstag

In a parliamentary system, winning seats was only the first step toward creating a government. The next step belonged to the president, who appointed a chancellor, or head of state, from among the members of the Reichstag. The new chancellor then faced the third challenge: putting together a governing majority. In a multiparty system, this was not an easy task.

The chancellor had to convince one or more parties to join his own in order to pass legislation. This involved high-level bargaining to give each party something it wanted in return for supporting the chancellor's legislative program. Failure to build a workable alliance could cripple the entire government.

If this should happen, responsibility fell back upon the president. He could invoke an emergency provision of the Weimar constitution to bypass the Reichstag and rule by decree, or he could dissolve the Reichstag and call for new elections.

In this case, Von Hindenburg reappointed Heinrich Brüning, hoping that new elections would change the composition of the Reichstag so that Brüning could put together a coalition. Instead, the balance of power shifted in the other direction, making a parliamentary majority impossible.[1] The Nazis' showing had played a major role in creating this impasse.

## A Bid for Respectability

As Hitler had vowed after Landsberg, he had achieved these gains legally. Two days after the election, he spoke out on its significance.

> For us Parliament is not an end in itself, but merely a means to an end . . . we are not on principle a parliamentary party—that would be a contradiction of our whole outlook—WE ARE A PARLIAMENTARY PARTY BY COMPULSION, UNDER CONSTRAINT, AND THAT COMPULSION IS THE CONSTITUTION. The Constitution compels us to use this means. It does not compel us to wish for a particular goal, it only prescribes a way—a method, and, I repeat, we follow this way legally, in accordance with the Constitution: by the way laid down through the Constitution we advance towards the purposes which we have set before us.[2]

The Third Reich would not be based upon constitutions and legal systems, he said, but upon "blood, authority of personality, and a fighting spirit."[3] These few words restate familiar Nazi themes of racism, life-as-struggle, and the *Führerprinzip*, which Hitler now characterized as "authority of personality."

Hitler concluded with a resounding, but curiously empty, call to action: "Do not write on your banners the word 'Victory': today that word shall be uttered for the last time. Strike through the word 'Victory' and write once more in its place the word which suits us better—the word 'Fight.'"[4]

He offered no plan for attaining this victory, either for himself or for the audience. Thus, the call for action became a call for allegiance to Nazi "ideals" and to the person of the Führer.

Hitler's talent for propaganda and self-promotion did not translate into an ability for strategy, planning, or administration. His speeches used emotion-laden "trigger"

**67**

words, slogans, and stock phrases. He spoke to whip the audience into a frenzy, not to give information or make logical arguments. Many of his most rousing speeches were little more than strings of catchphrases, held together by his almost uncanny ability to inspire an audience. Inspiration alone was not enough to keep some of the more militant SA members operating within the law. Hitler sent for the one man who could get these street brawlers under control: Ernst Röhm. Though once stripped of all authority and banished from the party, Röhm returned at the Führer's summons. On January 5, 1931, Hitler's old comrade-in-arms became chief of staff for the SA.

## An Election and a Scandal

At the urging of Joseph Goebbels and others, Hitler decided to run for president against the incumbent. His challenger was: eighty-five-year-old war hero and living legend Field Marshal Paul von Hindenburg.

In order to become a presidential candidate, Hitler had to take care of a rather embarrassing detail: He was not a German citizen. He had renounced his Austrian citizenship in 1925, but never applied to Germany.

He discovered that the quickest and easiest way to become a German citizen was to accept a position in the civil service, thus gaining automatic citizenship. Hitler's backers arranged a temporary job for him. So it was that Adolf Hitler briefly became what his father had always wanted him to be: a civil servant.

On March 13, 1932, Hitler won enough votes to deny President von Hindenburg an absolute majority and force a run-off election. During this second campaign, Hitler's opponents unearthed frankly homosexual correspondence between Ernst Röhm and another man. They hoped that the resulting scandal would derail Hitler's bid for political respectability.

That Ernst Röhm was a homosexual came as no surprise to Hitler; he had known all along and chosen to ignore it.[5] Many of his advisors felt he could not afford to continue looking the other way. This was a time in Germany when homosexuality was widely regarded as both a crime and a sin.

Hitler needed Röhm, and so he decided to go against advice and keep him in his position. He did not publicly acknowledge Röhm's homosexuality; he simply ignored it, saying that a man's private life was his own business so long as it did not interfere with the goals of the party.

The scandal died away, apparently with little effect on the election. Though Von Hindenburg won his majority, Hitler's strong showing thrust him into the limelight of the national political scene.

## Hard Bargains

Von Hindenburg's first order of business was appointing Franz von Papen as chancellor. Von Papen brought a certain aristocratic elegance to the job, but he did not have the backing to put together a governing majority in the Reichstag. This left Von Hindenburg with no choice but to dissolve the Reichstag and call for new elections.

To avoid yet another failure, Von Papen sought an alliance with Hitler and his National Socialists. Hitler agreed to support a government led by Von Papen but made it clear that he would not be content for long with a subordinate role: "I regard your Cabinet only as a temporary solution," he told the startled Von Papen, vowing to "continue my efforts to make my party the strongest in the country" so that the "Chancellorship will then devolve on me."[6]

Relying on Nazi cooperation, President von Hindenburg set new elections for July 31. The Nazis won 230 seats, becoming the largest party in the Reichstag. This surprisingly good showing meant that Hitler no longer needed Franz von Papen. He promptly reneged on his promise of support and demanded the chancellorship for himself.

President von Hindenburg would not hear of appointing the man he scornfully called the "[Austrian] corporal."[7] When Von Papen again failed to build a governing coalition, he resigned in favor of Kurt von Schleicher, a career army officer.

Schleicher tried to work around Hitler by offering the vice-chancellorship to number-two Nazi Gregor Strasser. Hitler threw a tantrum when Strasser asked him to support, or at least tolerate, a Schleicher cabinet. There would be no toleration, no cooperation, no compromise with Schleicher or anyone else, Hitler claimed.

Unreasonable as it seemed, even Strasser's personal friends supported Hitler's position. This impasse brought Strasser to a personal crisis. Like his brother Otto before him, Gregor Strasser realized that he could no longer continue to follow Adolf Hitler.

On December 8, Strasser resigned all his party offices. A furious Adolf Hitler condemned him as a traitor, dismantled the organizational structures he had created, removed his supporters from their posts, and generally tried to blot his name from party history.

## Chancellor Adolf Hitler

Without Nazi backing, Schleicher fared no better than Von Papen in building a government. Having run out of both options and ideas, Schleicher resigned the chancellorship on January 28, 1933.

Franz von Papen stepped back into the picture with a new plan: appoint Hitler as a figurehead chancellor, with Von Papen himself as vice-chancellor. With his crowd appeal, Hitler could deliver the masses, while Von Papen worked behind the scenes, exercising the real power. On that basis the president agreed, and so at midday on January 30, 1933, Adolf Hitler took the oath of office as chancellor of Germany.

Even among ardent nationalists and racists, there were those who feared what Hitler's rise to power might mean for Germany. Among the most outspoken were former comrades whom Hitler had betrayed in one way or another.

General Erich Ludendorff well knew the price of dealing with the new chancellor. This man who had marched with Hitler in the Beer Hall Putsch, only to be discarded later, sent an ominous warning to Von Hindenburg: "I prophesy to you this evil man [meaning Hitler] will plunge our Reich into the abyss and will inflict immeasurable woe on our nation."[8]

## The Enabling Act

Though only a few saw the warning signs, Ludendorff's prediction began coming true in the first weeks of Hitler's chancellorship. Hitler quickly got down to the business of consolidating his position. To do that, he needed a crisis, a clear and present danger that seemed to threaten the very existence of the German nation. He got it on the night of February 27, 1933, when fire gutted the Reichstag building.

Marinus van der Lubbe, a young communist sympathizer from Holland, was found inside the building. He readily admitted setting the fire and claimed that he had acted alone. The confession did not stop speculation on both sides of the political spectrum.

Some of Hitler's enemies thought that the fire was a Nazi operation, meant to create an issue for the upcoming elections. Hitler claimed that it was nothing less than the opening salvo of a communist revolution.

He called for immediate action to protect Germany from a communist takeover. The next day, an emergency "Decree

**71**

„Nimmer wird das Reich zerstöret – wenn ihr einig seid und treu"

1 Nationalsozialisten

For the Protection of People and State" suspended civil rights indefinitely and gave the Reich government new power over the previously autonomous states.

In the March 5 elections, voters swung sharply right. The Nazis became the largest party by far with 288 seats, or 44 percent of the Reichstag. Hitler was able to build a governing majority by making alliances with conservative nationalists. Immediately after forming this coalition, he authorized wholesale arrests of communists, socialists, trade-unionists, and other left-wingers.

The numbers were staggering. In a few short weeks, the Nazis arrested twenty-five thousand people in Prussia alone, with another ten thousand in Bavaria.[9] It happened in other German states as well. These political prisoners were not put into the regular prison system. The Nazis built concentration camps for them, beginning with Dachau, which opened on March 22, 1933.

Just two days later, Hitler used the mass arrests as "proof" of Germany's continuing danger. To combat that danger, he asked the Reichstag for an enabling act that would allow him dictatorial powers for a period of four years.

With passage of the Enabling Act, the Reichstag essentially put itself out of a job. It adjourned *sine die*—indefinitely, without naming a date for reconvening. By surrendering its rights as a legislative body, the Reichstag put an end to Weimar democracy and opened the way for what would be called the Führer State.

..................................................................................................................................................................

**When Hitler became chancellor, he played a secondary role to the legendary president Paul von Hindenburg. In English, the poster's caption reads, "The Reich will never be destroyed when you stay united and loyal."**

**73**

**6**

# The Making of
# the Führer

The Enabling Act allowed Adolf Hitler to begin transforming his private notions into public policy. It did not, however, give him an entirely free hand. Though the Reichstag suspended regular sessions, it did not disband. Hitler could still lose his governing majority if the conservatives broke away from his coalition government. He could still be dismissed by President von Hindenburg.

Under these circumstances, he avoided inflammatory speeches and street violence. He concentrated on creating a "national community" through a process that came to be known as *Gleichschaltung*, "coordination" or "alignment."[1] It referred to bringing the German people into line with National Socialist values through "political purification [and] a thorough moral purging of the body corporate of the nation."[2]

### *Gleichschaltung* and the Nazification of Germany

Hitler spoke against "the splitting up of the nation into groups with irreconcilable views," claiming that "only the creation of a real national community, rising above the interests and differences of rank and class. . . . [could produce] a solidarity of views in the German body corporate . . ."[3]

Gleichschaltung would coordinate every part of national life. It would create a monolithic political and legal structure, fostering tight control of the media, the arts, education, and daily life in a society shaped by "blood and race."[4]

Historian Edgar Feuchtwanger pointed out that the word Gleichschaltung was

> . . . a way of glossing over the threat of terror and violence that compelled individuals and organisations [sic] to come to heel. People could say that their organisations had been *gleichgeschaltet* (aligned, co-ordinated), when what had really happened was that former colleagues, who had become politically or racially inconvenient, had been brutally thrown out and often subjected to physical violence.[5]

This was the other side of Gleichschaltung; it drew a line between those who were "worthy" to become part of the national community and those who were not. Aryans and western Europeans of kindred blood could belong unless they had genetic defects or disabilities such as mental retardation or mental illness. Jews and people of color could not belong under any circumstances.

## Excluding Jews: The Beginning

In the first weeks of Hitler's chancellorship, militant anti-Semites began calling for immediate action against the Jews. Hitler wavered and worried, then announced a nationwide boycott of Jewish businesses, beginning on April 1 and continuing indefinitely. He put Julius Streicher in charge of an organizing committee and assigned publicity duties to his newly appointed minister for popular enlightenment and propaganda, Joseph Goebbels.

Having set the boycott into motion, Hitler meant to back away from the project and turn his attention to other matters. He did not get the chance. The boycott promptly ran into determined opposition from within the party leadership and from advisors such as banker Hjalmar Schacht and Foreign Minister Konstantin von Neurath. They warned of reprisal boycotts from the United States and several European nations. That, they told the Führer, could destroy the already weakened German economy.

Apparently, Hitler realized that he had gone too far. However, he could not bring himself to back down completely. That would involve admitting error; something he did not want to do. He finally settled on a face-saving maneuver: limiting the boycott to one day, with a proviso that it would begin again on April 5 unless foreign threats of boycott against Germany had been retracted.

On April 1, storm troopers took up positions in front of Jewish shops, businesses, and professional offices. The immediate effect was nowhere near what Hitler had wanted it to be. In some places, the boycott scarcely worked at all, as people ignored the scowling SA guards to patronize their favorite shops. The fifth of April came and went without so much as a mention of the word *boycott*.

In spite of poor results, the boycott had a lasting effect on Germany. As the first nationwide, government-sponsored action against the Jews, it gave official sanction to anti-Jewish measures.

## The "Aryan Paragraph"

Hitler's deadline for resuming the boycott came and passed without incident, but he quickly struck out at the Jews in another way. On April 7, the infamous "Aryan Paragraph" first appeared in the "Law for the Restoration of the Professional Civil Service."

Under the terms of this law, Jews were summarily dismissed from civil service positions. For purposes of enforcement, officials needed criteria for establishing who was, and who was not, a Jew. Though Hitler had long insisted that Jews were a race rather than a religious or cultural group, he could not find racial criteria for distinguishing them from non-Jews.

He fell back on the time-honored test of religion and culture: A Jew was someone who had even one Jewish parent or grandparent. To make the task of identification easier, employees bore the burden of proving their Aryan descent in order to keep their jobs.

The Aryan Paragraph became a tool for systematically removing Jews from German national life. For example, it was invoked to ban Jews from becoming lawyers, doctors, or dentists, and to restrict Jewish admission to German schools or universities.

## Propaganda and the Hitler Myth

By using race as a propaganda tool, Hitler was able to portray Jews as evil and dangerous beings while building his own legend as a tireless defender of the Aryan "master race." In manipulating public opinion, he had the help of propaganda minister Joseph Goebbels. Together, they crafted an image of superhuman strength, heroism, and wisdom, along with deep love for the German nation and the German people.

Hitler himself, ever conscious of his own public image, had laid the groundwork—keeping his past and his personal life shrouded in mystery, taking care not to let himself appear ridiculous or even ordinary. He never went swimming because his body was too pale and soft, never danced because

**77**

he might appear clumsy, never took part in sports because losing would be a public disgrace.

He built an image for himself in the same way he built an image for the Nazi movement. He blended fantasy with fact until separating the myth from the man and the propaganda from the politics became all but impossible.

When Hitler discussed propaganda in *Mein Kampf*, he was also describing his own habits of mind. He did not analyze political issues or military strategies; he reduced them to simplistic formulas, ignoring inconvenient facts or tailoring them to suit his needs:

> The function of propaganda is . . . not to weigh . . . the rights of different people, but exclusively to emphasize the one right which it has set out to argue for. Its task is not to make an objective study of the truth . . . and then set it before the masses with academic fairness; its task is to serve our own right, always and unflinchingly.

The attitude of the masses, Hitler said, is not based upon "sober reasoning," but upon "emotion and feeling. . . . And this sentiment is not complicated, but very simple and all of a piece. It does not have multiple shadings; it has a positive and a negative; love or hate, right or wrong, truth or lie, never half this way and half that way, never partially . . ."[6]

## Settling Old Accounts

Though Hitler's ability for rational analysis left much to be desired, he did have a good sense of political timing. As soon as he had consolidated his position as chancellor, he began preparing for the next step: becoming absolute dictator when President von Hindenburg died. To do that, he needed to have everything in place, then move quickly and ruthlessly at the proper time. He could not hope to do this without support from the military. Even in the midst of political victories and public adulation, getting that support would not be easy. The generals, with their aristocratic titles and long military tradition, were not anxious to follow a former corporal, especially one who had his own private "army" of street brawlers.

Since returning to command, Ernst Röhm had built the SA into a formidable unit. He made it painfully clear that he considered the SA Germany's army of the future. In a letter to General Walter von Reichenau, the Reich minister of war, Röhm made an unwise statement: "I regard the Reichswehr [army] now only as a training school for the German people. The conduct of war, and therefore of mobilization as well, in the future is the task of the SA."[7]

Many party leaders decided that Röhm had to go, but convincing Hitler to move against his old comrade-in-arms was a difficult task. Reinhard Heydrich, a young and ambitious SS man, was assigned to investigate Röhm's activities. He claimed that Röhm and the hated Gregor Strasser were secretly collaborating to overthrow Hitler. For extra measure, he carefully documented Röhm's secret life as a homosexual.

Hitler waffled this way and that, caught between public opinion and a loyal, if troublesome, comrade-in-arms. Everyone expected a decision; he knew that, but this was a complex situation, and he had never been good at complexities. Not until he realized Röhm and the SA stood between him and total power did he order a purge.

## The Night of Long Knives

On the night of June 29–30, 1934, SS killing squads tracked down their former comrades in the SA. Hitler himself undertook the task of arresting Ernst Röhm, whose last name is also sometimes spelled "Roehm." According to an eyewitness,

> Hitler entered Roehm's bedroom alone with a whip in his hand. Behind him were two detectives with pistols

**79**

at the ready. He spat out the words; "Roehm, you are under arrest."

Roehm's doctor comes out of a room and to our surprise he has his wife with him. I hear Lutze putting in a good word for him with Hitler. Then Hitler walks up to him, greets him, shakes hand [sic] with his wife and asks them to leave the hotel, it isn't a pleasant place for them to stay in, that day.

Now the bus arrives. Quickly, the SA leaders are collected . . . and walk past Roehm under police guard. Roehm looks up from his coffee sadly and waves to them in a melancholy way. At last Roehm too is led from the hotel. He walks past Hitler with his head bowed, completely apathetic.[8]

Hitler whipped himself into a frenzy over the arrest. To him, confronting Ernst Röhm was an act of utmost valor. Hours later, he was still hyperactive and unfocused. The only person his adjutant, or administrative assistant, could think to call was the architect Albert Speer.

Speer was becoming part of Hitler's inner circle, due largely to his talent in a field that was one of Hitler's secret passions. Speer later recalled the urgency in the adjutant's voice and the strange nature of his request: "Have you any new [architectural] designs? If so, bring them here!"

There was no need to ask what was happening; Speer already knew. Like a parent dealing with an unruly child, the adjutant was trying to distract Hitler with one of his pet interests. Speer grabbed a handful of sketches and went straightaway, finding exactly what he had expected to find:

Hitler was extremely excited and, as I believe to this day, inwardly convinced that he had come through a great danger. Again and again he described how he had forced his way into the Hotel Hanselmayer in Wiessee—not forgetting, in the telling, to make a show of his courage: "we were unarmed, imagine, and didn't know whether or not those swine might have armed guards to use

German soldiers march through Imst, Austria, in March 1938. Hitler had just taken over the country.

against us.". . . Evidently, he believed that his personal action had averted a disaster at the last minute: "I alone was able to solve this problem. No one else."[9]

Two SS men went to Röhm's cell. By personal order of the Führer, they placed a loaded gun on the table and left him alone. The meaning of this was clear. It was a common practice to give a valiant enemy the option of suicide.

Röhm, however, refused to accept this gesture from Hitler. If he was to die, then it would be by Hitler's hand and not his own. The SS men took aim and fired.

## The Killing Spree

Decimating the SA leadership was not enough for Hitler and the SS. They also wanted to settle accounts with some old political enemies. The "hit list" that doomed Ernst Röhm also included Hitler's longtime rival Gregor Strasser and General Kurt von Schleicher, the former chancellor whose scheming had nearly cost Hitler his chance at national office.

The executions of Strasser and Schleicher were especially brutal. Strasser was thrown into a cell with no place to hide while riflemen took potshots at him. They delivered the killing shot after growing tired of the "game." Schleicher and his wife were asleep in their own home when an SS execution squad burst into the bedroom and shot them where they lay.

In an impromptu program of damage control, Hitler met with his cabinet, spoke to the Reichstag, and took special pains to seek the approval of President von Hindenburg. The efforts paid off. Such was the fear of Röhm and the Brownshirts that the cabinet passed a retroactive law, legalizing the purge. The ministers of justice and the army endorsed it, as did President Hindenburg himself.

By eliminating Röhm and breaking the power of the SA, the Night of Long Knives removed the last obstacle to army endorsement of Adolf Hitler. It also marked the beginning of a new and expanded role for the SS. Under the direction of onetime chicken farmer Heinrich Himmler, it would become Hitler's instrument of terror, ferreting out enemies of the Reich and carrying out the Final Solution.

## Unprecedented Power

Just four weeks after the SA purge, the last obstacle to Hitler's dictatorship lay dying. In keeping with protocol, Hitler visited the bedside of President Paul von Hindenburg. After paying proper respects, Hitler met with his cabinet to pass a law combining the offices of Chancellor and President into one.

Hindenburg died the next day, and the mantle of leadership fell to Hitler. He had already chosen a title for himself: "Führer and Reich Chancellor." General Werner von Blomberg, in his capacity as Reich minister of war, endorsed Hitler's new status with an unprecedented move; by his order, soldiers all over Germany took what came to be known as "the Führer oath." It replaced the traditional army oath of allegiance to "people and country" with a vow to "render unconditional obedience to the Fuehrer of the German Reich and people, Adolf Hitler, Supreme Commander of the Wehrmacht."[10]

This was one of the earliest uses of the term *Wehrmacht* for the combined armed forces (army, navy, air force) of the Reich. To this oath from the military, Hitler wanted to add a resounding vote of confidence from the entire German people.

He did this on August 19, with a plebiscite: a direct vote in which the electorate approves or disapproves a proposal. Almost 90 percent of German voters approved combining the two offices, an overwhelming mandate that brought Adolf Hitler to the pinnacle of power.

**83**

Outside of Germany, people did not seem to know what to make of that mandate, nor of the man himself. On the day of the plebiscite, the *New York Times* reported that

> Eighty-nine and nine-tenths per cent of the German voters endorsed in yesterday's plebiscite Chancellor Hitler's assumption of greater power than has even been possessed by any other ruler in modern times. . . . The German people were asked to vote whether they approved the consolidation of the offices of President and Chancellor in a single Leader-Chancellor personified by Adolf Hitler. By every appeal known to skillful politicians and with every argument to the contrary suppressed, they were asked to make their approval unanimous. . . .
>
> The endorsement gives Chancellor Hitler, who four years ago was not even a German citizen, dictatorial powers unequaled in any other country, and probably unequaled in history since the days of Genghis Khan. He has more power than Joseph Stalin in Russia, who has a party machine to reckon with; more power than Premier Mussolini of Italy who shares his prerogative with the [king]; more than any American President every dreamed of.
>
> No other ruler has so widespread power nor so obedient and compliant subordinates [sic]. The question that interests the outside world now is what Chancellor Hitler will do with such unprecedented authority.[11]

## Working Toward the Führer

Even with his dictatorial powers, Hitler could not entirely ignore public opinion, especially not within the Nazi party, which was still his power base. The party rally of September 1934 presented a tremendous challenge; it was the first major gathering of Nazis since the Röhm purge.

Hitler prepared himself to win back any disaffected SA members. He had grandeur and pageantry enough to distract

# Dietrich Bonhoeffer

Theologian Dietrich Bonhoeffer was born on February 4, 1906. Dietrich took an early interest in theology, proving to be an adept—even brilliant—student. When Hitler came to power in 1933, Bonhoeffer was teaching theology in Berlin. He witnessed the changes in German life as the Nazis tightened their grip on power.

Those changes provoked a moral and spiritual crisis for the young theologian. He first limited his concerns to Christians of Jewish background. Nazis and Nazi sympathizers within the church wanted to ban "non-Aryans" from the ministry and other positions of church leadership. This went against church teaching about the fundamental equality of all Christians, regardless of their background.

Bonhoeffer later addressed the broader moral and human rights issues of the Final Solution. He spoke out so boldly that he soon ran afoul of the Nazi establishment. In April 1943, the Gestapo arrested and imprisoned Bonhoeffer. Two years later, on April 9, 1945, he was hanged at the Flossenburg concentration camp, just fourteen days before it was liberated by American troops.

even the most militant of his followers and a ready "explanation" for the excesses of the Night of Long Knives: ". . . you couldn't possibly know the whole story," he told former Röhm staffer Max Jüttner. "Röhm and Schleicher intended to make a Putsch against me and it had to be averted. I wanted to have these matters examined before a regular court, but events overwhelmed me and many SA leaders were shot without my consent. Because of all the world publicity I took the blame."[12]

Technically, this may have been true; Hitler gave the general order, but he kept his distance from the actual killings. That allowed him to shift a great deal of the responsibility to unnamed "others," while giving the impression that he had been blamed unfairly.

He became an expert at doing this, relying upon the German people to give him the benefit of the doubt, blaming acts of injustice, brutality, or wanton cruelty on underlings who exceeded their orders. "If the Führer only knew about this" became a familiar phrase throughout the Nazi era.

To further insulate himself from criticism and awkward questions, Hitler created a web of mystery around his person, keeping friends and enemies alike off-kilter and unsure of their ground. This constant confusion set him above the fray. It kept subordinates scrambling to figure out what he wanted, and opponents scrambling to figure out how far he would go to get it.

It also shifted responsibility for policy decisions from the Führer to his underlings, creating a safeguard that today might be called "plausible deniability." He disguised his motives and intentions, said one thing but did another, and made solemn promises he never intended to keep. He was unapologetically secretive about even small matters.

After the war, General Franz Halder would recall a particularly revealing conversation, in which the Führer told him to "take note of one thing from the start, that you will never discover my thought and intentions until I am giving my orders." When Halder responded that military strategists were used to working together, Hitler dismissed the idea with a wave of his hand: "No. Things are done differently in politics. You will never learn what I am thinking and those who boast most loudly that they know my thought, to such people I lie even more."[13]

To enhance this confusion, Hitler issued broad policy statements instead of specific commands, leaving his subordinates to fill in the details as they went along. Prussian state official Werner Willikens coined a term to describe this process: "working toward the Führer."

Willikens asserted that

> the Führer can only with great difficulty order from above everything that he intends to carry out sooner or later. Every loyal follower should therefore see that he "works toward the Führer."
>
> Very often . . . it has been the case that individuals . . . have waited for commands and orders. . . . [today] it is the duty of every single person to attempt, in the spirit of the Führer, to work towards him. Anyone making mistakes will come to notice it soon enough. But the one who works correctly towards the Führer along his lines and towards his aim will . . . have the finest reward of one day . . . attaining the legal confirmation of his work.[14]

Working toward the Führer was not an easy thing to do. First, dedicated Nazis had to identify Hitler's aims, replace their own ideas with his, and then devise methods of putting his principles into action. The process would bind them ever closer to Hitler—and to his dark vision for the German people.

# Love, Lebensraum, and Power Struggles

Having achieved the pinnacle of power and Nazified Germany with the policy of *Gleichschaltung*, Hitler was ready for new conquests. He wanted to turn the German people into a "master race" and the German nation into a mighty empire that would rule the world for a thousand years. To achieve these goals, he would devise murderous "racial hygiene" programs, build up the German military in defiance of the Versailles Treaty, and grab foreign territory to create lebensraum, or "living space," for the German nation. Hitler began his territorial acquisitions with the Saar, a strip of land known for its rich deposits of coal. It had belonged to Germany until the Treaty of Versailles placed it under League of Nations administration for a period of fifteen years. When that period ended in 1935, Saarlanders could choose to remain under league control, become part of France, or rejoin Germany.

To retake the Saarland, Hitler did not have to launch an invasion, only win an election. He put Joseph Goebbels to work, saturating the region with propaganda. It proved to be effective: On January 13, 1935, an overwhelming majority of Saarlanders decided for Germany. A mood of jubilation spread throughout the country. Many saw it as a process of healing, of Germany moving past defeat to begin reclaiming its place in the world.

The strength of that reaction confirmed Hitler's feeling that the time had come for a new and bolder move against the very substance of the Versailles Treaty. On March 16, 1935, he announced to the world press that Germany would rearm, expanding the army from its legal limit of 100,000 troops to 550,000 and forming a new German air force as well.

## On Hitler's Mountain

While Hitler had developed a gambler's instinct for political risk-taking, he was still inept in personal relationships. Even people in his inner circle were more like followers than friends. They gave him the constant audience he needed, while also helping to insulate him from the outside world.

This "insider" status came at a price. This was especially true at his mountain retreat above the town of Berchtesgaden. There, guests lived in Hitler's constant presence, and many found this a difficult thing to do.

Life at Berchtesgaden revolved completely around the Führer. According to frequent guest Albert Speer, living in Hitler's presence meant getting to bed at two or three o'clock in the morning and sleeping until nearly noon. It meant long afternoon meals and even longer evening ones. It meant watching movies and talking until

> some members of the company, in spite of all their efforts to control themselves, could no longer repress their yawns. But the social occasion dragged on in monotonous, wearing emptiness . . . until at last Eva

**89**

Braun had a few words with Hitler and was permitted to go upstairs. Hitler would stand up about a quarter of an hour later, to bid his company goodnight. . . . After a few days of this I was seized by what I called at the time "the mountain disease." That is, I felt exhausted and vacant from the constant waste of time. . . . As a favored permanent guest . . . I could not withdraw from these evenings, agonizing as they were, without appearing impolite. . . . During Hitler's longer stays at [Berchtesgaden] the only way to save oneself was to flee to Berlin.[1]

One person who could not get away was Eva Braun. Hitler kept her under tight control, as he had done with his niece Geli. He decided when Eva could be present at his side, and when she could not. Even in the informal atmosphere of the mountain, she could never forget her inferior status. Albert Speer observed that she

was allowed to be present during visits from old party associates. She was banished as soon as other dignitaries of the Reich, such as cabinet ministers, appeared at table. Even when Goering [Göring] and his wife came, Eva Braun had to stay in her room. Hitler obviously regarded her as socially acceptable only within strict limits.[2]

In part, the standards of the time imposed those limits; heads of state did not flaunt their mistresses in public. Eva Braun knew this as well as anyone and seems to have accepted it readily enough. What she could not accept was living in constant uncertainty: "I haven't had a good word from him in three months . . ." she wrote in her diary for May 28, 1935, and later concluded that "the uncertainty is more terrible than a sudden ending of it all."[3]

Shortly after that, she took an overdose of sleeping pills, but her sister found her in time. Some people suspected that she never intended to kill herself, only to frighten Hitler into paying more attention to her. If so, the demonstration worked; Hitler moved her in to an apartment close to his own and began calling more regularly.

## Hitler and the Nuremberg Laws

In addition to the difficulties with Eva Braun, the spring and summer of 1935 brought a political crisis. Militants from what was left of the SA roamed the streets in vigilante bands, looking for Jews to attack. Their lust for violence provoked outrage from the businessmen and industrialists Hitler needed in the Nazi fold.

Most of that outrage was based on economic concerns rather than humanitarian ones. Lawlessness in the streets disrupted the social order and drained the economy. The leaders of business and industry wanted a more rational and "civilized" approach to the Jewish problem.

In response, Hitler presented the infamous "Nuremberg Laws" at the annual party rally in September 1935. The "Law for the Protection of German Blood and German Honor" prohibited marriage and sexual relations between Jews and "citizens of German or kindred blood."[4] It also prohibited Jews from hiring German women under the age of forty-five as domestic servants. The "Reich Citizenship Law" stripped Jews of their German citizenship and subsequently their fundamental political rights.

These laws would be amended and expanded many times. They became a wall of words, slowly encircling the Jews and setting them apart. Much like Hitler's technically lawful seizure of power in 1933, the Nuremberg Laws changed the legal and political foundations of German society. Enforcement fell to various government agencies, allowing the Führer to stand apart from the murderous forces he had set into motion.

**91**

# Werner Klemperer

When Hitler came to power in 1933, actor Werner Klemperer was just thirteen years old. As a Jew, Otto, Werner's father, became a target of harassment and death threats. In March 1933, the family fled Nazi Germany, eventually ending up in Los Angeles, California.

Like other immigrant children, Werner had to learn a new language and new customs. In Germany, he would probably have followed his father into a musical career. In the United States, he decided to become an actor.

After studying at the famous Pasadena Playhouse, Werner Klemperer built a solid career, playing character parts in movies and onstage. Oddly enough, this refugee from Hitler's Germany often played Nazi characters. Directors found his bearing and manner ideal for these roles.

He worked steadily but remained largely unknown. Then in 1965, he found what would become his signature role, playing the commandant of a Nazi prisoner-of-war camp in a new television comedy: *Hogan's Heroes.* Klemperer's Colonel Wilhelm Klink was pompous, vain, and none-too-bright, a born loser who never once got the best of the Allied prisoners in his charge. In 1968 and again in 1969, Klemperer won the Emmy award for best supporting actor in a comedy series. After *Hogan's Heroes*, he continued his career as a working actor until his death on December 6, 2000.

## The International Hitler

After the Nuremberg rally, Hitler turned his attention to "international matters." For him, international matters sooner or later came down to the hated Versailles Treaty. He had pushed the boundaries of the treaty once, by announcing German rearmament.

Now he wanted to try an even bolder move: send German troops into the Rhineland, a strip of territory along the Rhine River in western Germany. This would violate two major international treaties: the Treaty of Versailles, which designated the Rhineland as a demilitarized zone, and the Treaty of Locarno, which reaffirmed that status in 1925.

Hitler's generals advised against it; too risky, they said. What if England, France, or one of the other nations involved in the treaties decided to fight back? Hitler did not have an answer to satisfy the generals; the operation was basically a bluff and he knew it.

Years later, he admitted as much to Albert Speer: "We had no army worth mentioning. . . . If the French had taken any action, we would have been easily defeated; our resistance would have been over in a few days. And what air force we had then was ridiculous. A few Junkers 52's from Lufthansa, and not even enough bombs for them."[5]

In spite of these weaknesses and in defiance of his generals, Hitler decided to go with his instincts. On the morning of March 7, 1936, German troops marched into the Rhineland. Hitler's sole concession to his advisors that did not agree with him was to order a fighting retreat at the first sign of military resistance.

Neither France, England, nor the League of Nations offered that resistance. Thus, Hitler's gamble paid off, increasing

Germany's territory and raising the Führer myth to even greater heights.

The enthusiastic response in Germany stunned foreign observers, who expected at least some public opposition. In the name of the German people, Hitler had broken treaties and launched a military adventure that might have triggered war. Still, Germany cheered.

For Hitler, this was a shining moment. In a single bold and dangerous gesture, he had backed down the Western democracies, reclaimed territory for Germany, and earned the adulation of the masses.

With this success, Hitler began to see himself in yet another role: the warrior-king whose word moved armies and whose tactical genius rivaled the likes of Charlemagne, Frederick the Great, and Napoléon. The Rhineland results practically guaranteed more such military adventures in the near future.

Hitler was eager to make valuable alliances with like-minded enemies of the Soviet Union and the Western democracies. A few months after retaking the Rhineland, he signed an anti-comintern (communist) pact with Japan and began building a political relationship with Italian dictator Benito Mussolini.

## The Führer's Plans

Hitler's boldness on the international scene bothered many leaders of the Wehrmacht, the combined armed forces of the Reich. After the Röhm purge of 1934 had neutralized the SA, the army supported Hitler in the mistaken notion that he could be controlled. When Hitler created the Nuremberg Laws, started the process of rearmament, and sent soldiers into the Rhineland, military leaders began to realize how wrong they had been.

At a meeting on November 5, 1937, some of them saw the cost of that error: Hitler meant to start a war. Military adjutant Colonel Friedrich Hossbach kept careful notes on the Führer's speech. The "Hossbach memorandum," as it came to be known, set forth Hitler's intentions for Czechoslovakia and Austria.

Germany needed lebensraum, Hitler said, and flatly stated that the problem "could only be solved by means of force." While admitting that military aggression "was never without attendant risk," the Führer made it clear that he would not hesitate to take that risk:

> Our first objective, in the event of our being embroiled in war, must be to overthrow Czechoslovakia and Austria. . . . the annexation of Czechoslovakia and Austria would mean an acquisition of foodstuffs for 5 to 6 million people. . . . The incorporation of these two States with Germany . . . [would be] a substantial advantage because it would mean shorter and better frontiers, the freeing of forces for other purposes, and the possibility of creating new units up to a level of about 12 divisions, that is, 1 new division per million inhabitants.[6]

Field Marshal Werner von Blomberg, war minister and commander in chief of the Wehrmacht, backed by General Werner von Fritsch, commander in chief of the army, spoke against risking war. The Wehrmacht was not ready, they said. Any attack on Czechoslovakia or Austria might bring Germany into conflict with Great Britain and France.

By Hitler's standards, his generals were becoming obstructionists—counseling him to slow down, think through strategies, avoid actions that might provoke a war that Germany could not hope to win. They were entirely too cautious for Hitler's taste.

## A Pair of Scandals

In January 1938, both Blomberg and Fritsch became involved in scandals that called their character and judgment into question. The Blomberg crisis began when the field marshal married a much younger woman from a working-class background. It was a small and quiet ceremony with Hitler and Hermann Göring serving as legal witnesses.

Shortly after the wedding, an anonymous caller reported that the new Frau Blomberg had a shady past. Not only had she posed for pornographic pictures taken by her Jewish lover, but she had also been arrested for prostitution.

Hitler was horrified. According to one story, he took seven baths in a single afternoon, seeking to purify himself because he had kissed the bride's hand.[7] Even if this account is not literally true, it illustrates the depth of the Führer's chagrin.

Blomberg had one chance to salvage his career; he had to annul, or cancel, his marriage on the grounds that his bride had committed fraud by concealing her past. To almost everyone's surprise, Blomberg refused to renounce his marriage. He simply submitted his resignation and took his new wife for an extended vacation in Italy.

In the ordinary course of events, General Fritsch would have been Blomberg's most likely successor in the war ministry. However, Hitler recalled a two-year-old accusation of homosexual activity with a young male prostitute. At the time, Hitler had regarded the report as baseless and ordered it destroyed. Now he ordered a new investigation.

It led to charges against Fritsch and Hitler's insistence that he step down immediately, without waiting for a verdict from the military court. The charges turned out to be a case of mistaken identity, involving an officer named Achim Frisch.

Hitler did not restore Fritsch to his post as commander in chief of the army. Instead, he used the Blomberg-Fritsch crisis in much the same way he once used the Röhm crisis—as an excuse for a purge of the ranks. Unlike the notorious "Night of Long Knives," the purge of 1938 was bloodless.

In quick succession, Hitler ordered fourteen senior generals to retire and reassigned forty other officers to different commands. He also replaced two important civilian officials: Foreign Minister Konstantin von Neurath with Joachim von Ribbentrop,[8] and Finance Minister Hjalmar Schacht with Walther Funk. Neither of the new appointees was as able as the man he replaced, but both had one invaluable trait: They would follow Hitler's orders without question or argument.

Hitler then proceeded to reorganize the entire command structure of the military. He abolished the office of war minister altogether and took over its functions himself. He then created a new organization: the Armed Forces High Command (German initials OKW), naming General Wilhelm Keitel as its commander. Actually, Keitel was little more than an office manager, attending to administrative details while Hitler made the command decisions.

## Hitler's Homecoming

In November 1937, Hitler had envisioned launching a war with the conquest of Austria and Czechoslovakia. As it turned out, he did not need to attack either country; blackmail and bullying did the job.

On February 12, 1938, Hitler summoned Chancellor Kurt von Schuschnigg to meet with him at Berchtesgaden. At that point, he browbeat the Austrian leader into appointing a Nazi, Arthur Seyss-Inquart, as minister of the interior.

Schuschnigg apparently knew that this was only the beginning. He tried to arrange a plebiscite on Austrian independence, but he had run out of time. On March 11, Hitler gave the order: German troops would invade Austria at dawn the next morning.

That evening, Chancellor Schuschnigg made a radio broadcast, explaining the situation: "This day has placed us in a tragic and decisive situation," he said.

> The German Government today handed to President Miklas an ultimatum, with a time limit, ordering him to nominate as chancellor a person designated by the German Government and to appoint members of a cabinet on the orders of the German Government, otherwise German troops would invade Austria. . . . President Miklas has asked me to tell the people of Austria that we have yielded to force since we are not prepared even in this terrible situation to shed blood. We have decided to order [Austrian] troops to offer no resistance.[9]

The next morning at dawn German troops marched over the border into Austria. As Chancellor Schuschnigg had promised, there was no resistance; in fact, crowds of Austrians lined the streets to cheer the *anschluss*, or annexation. This euphoria would not withstand the daily realities of Nazification, as Hitler gradually transformed Austria into a pale echo of the German Fatherland.

So the angry, impoverished young man who left Vienna as a failure returned in triumph. A cheering crowd packed the street in front of his hotel. Like an actor taking curtain calls, Hitler would appear on the balcony from time to time, sending the crowd into a frenzied burst of cheering.

Much as he had done in the Rhineland, Hitler presented the world with a *fait accompli*, or accomplished fact, gambling that the Western democracies would accept the situation rather than risk war. He was right; Great Britain and

Hitler was committed to the Nazification of Germany's young people. Here, he receives the salute of Hitler Youth members.

France, principal signers of the Versailles Treaty, were not ready to fight to enforce its terms.

## The Sudetenland: "Just One More Thing"

Relying on this determination to preserve the peace, Hitler set his sights on the next target: Czechoslovakia. He began with the Sudetenland, a region along the Czech-German border, which had a large population of ethnic Germans. They became his excuse for a German takeover.

He pressed his claim with promises of peace and threats of war. He claimed that "solving the Czech question" would satisfy "Germany's territorial claims in Europe." There would be no further demands. However, if the Czechs did not accept his terms by 2 P.M. on September 28, Germany would take the Sudetenland by force.

One war—the war of nerves—had already begun. While the world watched and waited, British Prime Minister Neville Chamberlain and French premier Edouard Daladier, along with Mussolini of Italy, met with Hitler in Munich, Germany. To the outside world, the Führer appeared to be in control, both of himself and the situation. American correspondent William L. Shirer chanced to see a very different view:

> I was having breakfast in the garden of the Dreesen Hotel, where Hitler is [staying], when the great man suddenly appeared, strode past me, and went down to the edge of the Rhine to inspect his river yacht. X, one of Germany's leading editors . . . nudged me: "Look at his walk!" On inspection it was a very curious walk indeed. In the first place, it was very ladylike. Dainty little steps. In the second place, every few steps he cocked his right shoulder nervously, his left leg snapping up as he did so. I watched him closely as he came back past us. The same nervous tic. He had ugly black patches under his eyes. I think the man is on the edge of a nervous breakdown.[10]

To the confusion of most everyone who dealt with him, Hitler could appear absolutely reasonable at times. He played on British Prime Minister Neville Chamberlain's desire to avoid war at almost any cost, reassuring him about Germany's peaceful intentions. All he wanted, he vowed, was this small strip of land, already heavily populated with Germans.

Taking him at his word, Chamberlain agreed. The two leaders, along with Edouard Daladier of France and Benito Mussolini of Italy, set forth terms in the "Munich Agreement." It ceded the Sudetenland to Germany and specified procedures for an orderly change of power. In return, Hitler promised not to violate the new Czech borders.

## Hitler and the Jewish Problem: Another Chapter

While Hitler focused on his international adventures and worked on strategies for gaining lebensraum, the years 1936–1937 were relatively calm for German Jews. Some Jews had begun to feel that the worst might be over.

Then came December 1937, and the beginning of a whole new series of anti-Semitic decrees. Hitler was already thinking ahead to war. He wanted to step up the pace of rearmament and also to rid the country of its "enemy within:" the Jews.

With the help of Hermann Göring, Hitler devised a way to take care of both problems at the same time. He would first strip Jews of their property, then force them out of the country.

According to government estimates, German-Jewish assets were worth more than 5 billion Reichsmarks (2 billion American dollars).[11] At a time when German consumers could buy a new car for as little as four hundred dollars,[12] 2 billion was a staggering amount of money. It would go a long way toward paying the cost of rearmament. Hitler wanted to complete the process as quickly as possible, so he ordered the SS to step up the pace of seizing property and expelling Jews.

**101**

One of those expulsions would trigger a nationwide outbreak of violence that left synagogues in flames, Jewish cemeteries desecrated, businesses vandalized, and people terrorized, beaten, and even killed. It started on October 28, 1938; the SS rounded up seventeen thousand Polish Jews who had been living in Germany, packed them into boxcars, and took them to the German-Polish border. Poland refused to admit this ragtag band of refugees, leaving them trapped at the border with nowhere to go.

## Kristallnacht: The Night of Broken Glass

Seventeen-year-old Herschel Grynszpan was living in Paris with an uncle when he learned that his parents were among those stranded at the German-Polish border. Grieved by his family's plight, and by the general treatment of Jews in Nazi Germany, Herschel Grynszpan decided to take some measure of revenge against the Nazis. On November 7, he walked into the German embassy and asked to see the ambassador. When the ambassador did not appear, Herschel Grynszpan took a gun from his pocket and shot the first official he saw: Ernst vom Rath.

Vom Rath died two days later, on November 9. Hitler and the rest of the Nazi leadership got the news in Munich, during their annual celebration of the 1923 Beer Hall Putsch. Hitler held a private discussion with Goebbels, then left the hall. Having the propaganda minister make the public announcement was Hitler's way of insulating himself from responsibility for his decision.[13]

Goebbels took the podium; there would surely be outbursts of anti-Semitic violence, he said. However, the Führer had "decided that such demonstrations are not to be prepared or organized by the party, but so far as they originate spontaneously, they are not to be discouraged either."[14]

To experienced Nazis, the message was clear: Do anything, but keep the party—and the Führer—out of it. In the privacy of his diary, Goebbels spoke more plainly:

> I reported to the Fuehrer and he decides (sic): the demonstrations should be allowed to continue. The police should retreat. Let the Jews get a taste of popular anger. He is right. I immediately instructed the party and police accordingly. . . . Driving to the hotel, windows are being smashed. Bravo. Bravo. The synagogues burn like big old huts. There is no danger to German property.[15]

Nazi functionary Walter Funk coined a name for the events of that November 1938: *Kristallnacht*, or the Night of Broken Glass. It referred to the shards of window glass that littered the streets after the attacks. Kristallnacht marked a turning point for anti-Semitic policies in Germany. According to political scientist Dr. Harvey R. Kornberg, it "demonstrated that a threshold had been crossed. Prior to Kristallnacht . . . acts of physical violence against the Jews had been exceptional and sporadic. Kristallnacht was a nationwide organized pogrom in which physical violence was a major part."[16]

It also marked another first: By Hitler's order, twenty thousand to thirty thousand Jewish men were arrested and sent to concentration camps. Unlike the prisoners already in the camps, the Jews were not arrested for political activity, but simply for the "crime" of being Jewish.

In the aftermath of Kristallnacht, Hitler decided that it was time to develop plans for "cleansing" Germany of all Jewish influence. He handed the task to Hermann Göring, who called a meeting of high-ranking Nazis for November 12, just three days after Kristallnacht.

Göring opened the conference with an announcement that he had received "a letter written on the Fuehrer's orders requesting that the Jewish question be now, once and for all, coordinated and solved one way or another."[17] The meeting of November 12, 1938, did not "solve" the Jewish question once and for all. However, it did produce a plan for the systematic Aryanization of Jewish business.

It also shifted the cost of Kristallnacht damages from the Nazi perpetrators to the Jewish victims. The committee decided that the government should confiscate insurance payments to Jews. It also levied a fine of one billion Reichsmarks on the Jewish community as a whole as punishment for the actions of one disturbed teenager.

## Czechoslovakia Again

Just four months after Kristallnacht and six months after signing the Munich Pact to guarantee Czechoslovakia's borders, Hitler did what he had promised not to do: He set out to bring Czechoslovakia under German control. In a variant of his fait accompli strategy, he met with Czech president Emil Hácha in Berlin and browbeat him into accepting a German protectorate.

On March 14, 1939, German troops stood ready to march into Prague. Czech army trucks drove through the streets of the city with loudspeakers blaring: "German soldiers will enter our native lands. These soldiers will enter Prague, they will occupy our nation. Our army will not resist."[18]

The Czechs did not resist and the Western democracies did not respond. Thus, Adolf Hitler added another bloodless coup to his list of achievements. It would soon prove to be a costly victory.

By breaking the Munich Agreement just six months after signing it, Hitler crossed an invisible line with British Prime Minister Neville Chamberlain. Chamberlain realized that his policy of appeasement, granting concessions to keep the peace, had failed.

Hitler did not realize that he had pushed too far. Instead of pulling back, he grew bolder in his demands. This time, Poland was his target. His advisors reminded him that England and France had promised to aid Poland in the event of an attack. Hitler was not impressed; they had also promised to aid Czechoslovakia. "Why should England fight?" he asked. "One does not die for an ally."[19] With that, Hitler plunged ahead, trusting that his instincts would not let him down.

# 8

# The Führer's War

Before invading Poland, Hitler wanted to be sure that the Soviet Union would stay out of the fight. That meant dealing with Soviet dictator Josef Stalin, a man who embodied the communist philosophy Hitler despised and who belonged to a people he had condemned as "subhuman."

Hitler made an ideological about-face, sending Foreign Minister Joachim von Ribbentrop to Moscow to conclude a nonaggression pact that would leave Germany free to attack Poland. On August 23, 1939, Ribbentrop and Soviet Foreign Commissar Vyacheslav M. Molotov signed the official agreement in a public ceremony.

They signed the infamous "secret protocols" of that agreement in private. Hitler and Stalin carved up Poland between them, agreeing that Germany would confine its operations to western Poland, leaving the east to Russia. Hitler was fairly generous in his terms, largely because he meant to break the treaty as soon as he no longer needed it.

## Last-Minute Maneuvers

Hitler envisioned a time when Russia's vast lands would provide lebensraum for German expansion. It was all a matter of time, he told his commanders. First Poland, later Russia, and this would not be traditional warfare. It would be blitzkrieg, "lightning war," fast and brutal, with no attempt to spare civilians: "As regards our conduct of the war," he told his commanders, "close your hearts to pity! Act brutally! Crush every living spark! . . . Might is right—so we must act with the greatest harshness." In his summation, Hitler made it clear that the immediate "military objective" was nothing less than "the wholesale destruction of Poland."[1]

Publicly, Hitler ridiculed the idea that Great Britain and France would go to war over Poland. Privately, he worried that they might do just that. He especially wanted the British on his side. Proposals and counterproposals went back and forth between London and Berlin. The British did not budge; instead of focusing on Hitler's demands, they explored peaceful means of settling Germany's conflict with Poland.

Hitler simply did not understand his repeated failures in dealing with Great Britain. When he learned that Birger Dahlerus, a Swedish friend of Hermann Göring's, had lived and worked in England, he plied the man with questions about the British.

The more he talked, the more agitated he became. According to Dahlerus, Hitler

> walked up and down saying, as though to himself, that Germany was irresistible and could defeat her adversaries by means of a rapid war. Suddenly he stopped, stared into space, and began talking as if in a trance: "If there should be a war, then I will build U-boats, build U-boats, build U-boats, U-boats, U-boats, U-boats . . ."
> It was like a record that had stuck, his voice becoming

**107**

> more and more indistinct as it died away. Then, suddenly, a spasm shook his body. He lifted his arms in the air and began to shriek, as though addressing a huge audience, but still staccato and disjointed: "I will build aircraft, build aircraft, aircraft . . . and I will destroy my enemies! War does not frighten me! . . . If the enemy can hold out for several years, I, with my power over the German people, can hold out one year longer. It is because of this that I know I am superior to all the others."[2]

Dahlerus was "horrified" by this odd and disconnected behavior on the part of a world leader and "equally horrified" that Göring "did not seem at all perturbed at Hitler's glassy eyes and unnatural voice."[3]

When Hitler slipped back into more normal behavior, he acted as if nothing at all had happened. Then he asked Dahlerus why he had never been able to make an agreement with the British.

The Swede hesitated for a moment, not wanting to trigger another outburst. Then he did something that few in Hitler's inner circle had the courage to do: He told the truth as he saw it. The British, he said, simply did not trust Hitler or his Nazi government.

Not long after this encounter with Dahlerus, Hitler gave up his efforts to negotiate with the British. He decided to rely on his old, tried-and-true formula: Strike hard and fast, present a fait accompli, and rely upon the British dread of war to carry the day. With the decision finally made, he set a new date for the invasion of Poland: September 1, 1939.

## The War No One Wanted

Hitler had promised to give "a propagandist reason for starting the war no matter whether it is plausible or not. The victor will not be asked afterward whether he told the truth or not. When starting and waging war it is not right that matters, but victory."[4]

At 12:40 P.M. on August 31, Hitler issued the final order: "Directive Number 1 for the Conduct of War." This set his "propagandist reason" into motion. German soldiers dressed a group of concentration camp prisoners in Polish uniforms, drugged them into unconsciousness, and transported them to a radio station just inside the German-Polish border. There, the "Polish invaders" were shot dead and left lying on the ground. While SS men dressed as Polish soldiers staged other "incursions" on German territory, the main body of troops massed on the border. At 4:45 A.M., they marched into Poland.

Nothing had prepared the Poles for the German onslaught; tanks, field artillery, and foot soldiers moved constantly forward, crushing everything in their path. Planes screamed down from the sky, attacking people and installations on the ground. In the harbor at Danzig, the battleship *Schleswig-Holstein* opened fire. Its eleven-inch guns wiped out a Polish garrison, along with more than eighty men.

Hitler felt sure that Great Britain and France would back down when they saw the devastating effect of blitzkrieg. This time, he was wrong. On September 3, Great Britain and France declared war on Germany, leaving Hitler to realize that he had finally pushed too far.

## The "Phony War"

The realization did not last. Hitler's blitzkrieg conquered Poland in just twenty-six days, and there was nothing Great Britain or France could do about it. According to Albert Speer, the Führer soon convinced himself that

> England and France had obviously declared war merely as a sham, in order not to lose face before the whole world. In spite of the declarations there would be no

**109**

fighting; he was convinced of that, he said. He therefore
ordered the Wehrmacht to remain strictly on the defensive. He felt that this decision of his showed remarkable
political acumen.[5]

Hitler kept faith in this belief by the simple tactic of
ignoring evidence to the contrary. "His illusions and wish-
dreams were a direct outgrowth of his unrealistic mode of
working and thinking," wrote Speer. "Hitler actually knew
nothing about his enemies and even refused to use the
information that was available to him. Instead, he trusted his
inspirations, no matter how inherently contradictory they
might be . . ."[6]

In the first seven months of the war, September 1939 to
April 1940, neither side launched a major offensive. There
was almost no action at all in France, where life went on in a
more-or-less normal fashion. People began to call it the
"phony war," or *sitzkrieg* ("sitting war").

On April 9, 1940, Hitler turned sitzkrieg back into
blitzkrieg by invading Denmark and Norway. One month
later, on May 10, he launched an attack on France, Belgium,
Luxembourg, and the Netherlands. Each fell in turn, with
France surrendering on June 22. There was no more talk about
a phony war; this one was for real.

## The Racial War

The people of Poland never thought the war was phony. To
them, it was always brutal, bloody, and painfully real.
Germany annexed part of western Poland to the Reich and
put the rest under an occupational government. In keeping
with the secret protocols between Hitler and Stalin, the
Soviet Union took over in the east. Thus, Poland ceased to
exist as a sovereign nation.

For Hitler, taking Poland was not only about conquest and lebensraum; it was about race. He considered Poles and other Slavic peoples to be "subhuman," racially inferior to Germans, and suited only for the lowest kind of manual labor. Occupied Poland, known as "General Government," was to become what Hitler called "a reservation for Poles, a huge Polish work camp."[7]

To make the Poles into docile and obedient laborers, Hitler warned that:

> We must be ruthlessly on our guard to prevent the emergence of any "Polish masters;" ... the Poles can only have one master, and that is the German ... therefore all representatives of the Polish intelligentsia should be eliminated. .... This sounds harsh, but such are the laws of life.[8]

On the strength of this order, German troops killed thousands of intellectuals, government officials, clergy, and nobility. Hitler meant to create a vacuum at the top, leaving the Polish nation leaderless, vulnerable, and therefore easy to control.

The treatment of Polish Jews was even worse. Hitler placed the SS in charge of the "Jewish problem" in Poland, leaving Heinrich Himmler and his second-in-command Reinhard Heydrich to develop and administer policies. The first step was to create ghettos in rundown neighborhoods of Polish cities. All the Jews in a particular area were forced to move into these grim, overcrowded neighborhoods. They became a ready pool of slave labor for various German concerns. Thousands died in the ghettos, from starvation, exposure, or epidemic disease.

For those who survived the ghettos, the Germans built concentration camps. Periodically, the SS would fill railroad boxcars with human cargo, bound for places with names like

Auschwitz, Stutthof, and Plaszow. In the early days of the war, these were not death camps. Though death was a daily reality for the inmates, the killing was not systematic. The order for the Final Solution had not yet been given.

## "Life Unworthy of Life"

In Germany itself, there were thousands of people whose supposed "Aryan blood" could not save their lives. They had mental retardation, mental illness, physical handicaps, or deformities. Hitler regarded them as "useless mouths"—people who used up resources but gave nothing in return.

He had long considered the idea of "mercy killings," or euthanasia (meaning literally "good death"), for such people. He dealt with it frankly in his *Second Book*, which was written in 1928 but not published until 1961. He wrote that

> nature, out of the multitude of creatures that are born, spares the few healthiest and most robust in the struggle for survival, man reduces the number of births but then tries to preserve the lives of all those who are born, regardless of their true value.

A better solution, he said, would be to "place no controls on the number of births but limit the number allowed to live." He cited ancient Sparta as an example of a civilization that was "capable of such a wise measure."

According to him, Sparta practiced "systematic racial preservation," thereby becoming "the first racialist state" in recorded history. He was referring to the practice of abandoning unwanted newborns to die. In his view, the "abandonment of sick, frail, deformed children—in other words, their destruction—demonstrated greater human dignity and was in reality a thousand times more humane than the pathetic insanity of our time, which attempts to preserve the lives of the sickest subjects . . ." and eventually ends up "breeding a race of degenerates burdened with illness."[9]

Hitler's ideas about "racial hygiene" came into focus in 1938, when the father of a severely disabled newborn presented Hitler with a test case for euthanasia. Little is known about the man or his family, except that the name was "Knauer" and the baby had multiple handicaps, including blindness, seizures, and probable mental retardation. A leg and part of an arm were missing.

The family doctors refused to kill the child, on the grounds that it was against the law. Not to be deterred, Knauer wrote directly to the Führer, seeking his permission to have the baby killed. Hitler sent Dr. Karl Brandt to evaluate the case, instructing him to approve the killing if the baby's condition was as bad as Knauer had claimed. Brandt examined the infant and gave permission for euthanasia.

This one case became the prototype for hundreds more. The program grew in stages: first newborns, then children up to three years of age, followed by older children, and finally adults. In October 1939, Hitler issued a secret directive, predated to September 1, the day the war began.

> Berlin, 1 Sept. 1939
>
> Reich Leader Bouhler and Dr. med. Brandt are charged with the responsibility of enlarging the competence of certain physicians, designated by name, so that patients who, on the basis of human judgment, are considered incurable, can be granted mercy death after a discerning diagnosis.
>
> (Signed)
>
> A. Hitler[10]

This was the limit of Hitler's direct participation in establishing the euthanasia program. He chose his people, set things into motion, then backed away, leaving underlings "working toward the Führer" to do the rest. He would step back into the picture in August 1941, to cancel the program after public outrage had made it into a political liability.

## The Battle of Britain

After setting the euthanasia program into motion, Hitler turned back to the war. By the summer of 1940, he had conquered Western Europe from Germany's borders to the beaches of northern France. Now only the English Channel stood between him and Great Britain. He could not mount a land invasion, because Germany lacked amphibious transports to carry soldiers and equipment across the channel and land them on the shore. He decided to turn the operation over to Hermann Göring's Luftwaffe, the German Air Force. Their job was to pound the British into submission so that Germany could conquer England without the need for a full-scale amphibious landing.

In July 1940, the Luftwaffe began bombing military and industrial targets in England. Though the British Royal Air Force (RAF) was outnumbered, its Spitfire fighter planes were faster and more maneuverable than the German Stukas. The British not only held their own but inflicted heavy losses on the enemy.

To counter these losses, Hitler decided to use a different tactic; instead of using the bombers as weapons of war, he would use them as instruments of terror. In September, he ordered Göring to stop the daylight bombing of military

**The Luftwaffe, Germany's Air Force, bombed every part of Poland during the blitzkrieg that began World War II.**

**114**

targets. Instead, the Luftwaffe would make night raids on British cities. Thus began what became known as the Blitz.

In London and other British cities, people slept in subway tunnels or other underground shelters. Parents sent their children to the country for safety's sake. By daylight, the English people went about their ordinary lives as best they could. Neither the leaders nor the people of Great Britain called for surrender.

By the end of October, even Hitler had to admit that the Blitz simply was not working; it was also weakening the Luftwaffe. The RAF had shot down 650 German planes. He ordered the Luftwaffe to stand down and postponed the land invasion of England. The postponement turned out to be a cancellation, as Hitler turned his attention back to the east.

## Code Name Barbarossa

Ultimately, his target in the east was the Soviet Union. However, he first attacked the Balkans, reasoning that the conquest of Yugoslavia and Greece would eliminate any threat from the southeastern border of the Soviet Union. The Germans were as brutal in Yugoslavia as they planned to be in Russia. They slaughtered thousands of civilians, especially Jews. Of Yugoslavia's prewar population of eighty thousand Jews, only fifteen thousand would survive.[11]

This was only a prelude to the carnage of Operation Barbarossa, Germany's war on the Soviet Union. By its very nature, war produces atrocities of various kinds: the torture of prisoners, the slaughter of innocent civilians, the wanton destruction of entire communities. In Operation Barbarossa, such savagery was not an unfortunate excess of war; it was part of the plan.

Hitler laid the groundwork weeks before the invasion, with orders to both the SS and the Wehrmacht. He assigned

## Heinrich Himmler

The man who would build Hitler's SS into an empire of its own was the son of a Munich schoolmaster. The young Heinrich Himmler was not a standout, nor did he seem especially ambitious or power hungry. He studied agriculture at the Munich Technical High School, sold fertilizer for a time, then tried his hand at poultry farming. He did not succeed in either activity.

This soft-spoken young man with the rounded, undistinguished face looked more like a bank clerk than a killer. Perhaps this is why many regarded him as the most sinister of Hitler's close associates. Neither his appearance nor his manner matched his behavior.

Heinrich Himmler had no stomach for the mass murder he ordered. The only Einsatzgruppen execution he witnessed made him violently ill. That did not stop him from carrying out his orders from the Führer. He continued to order the executions and to praise the killers for having "remained decent fellows" in spite of the slaughter.[12]

Himmler and the SS to "wage a war of extermination against Bolshevism and Jewry."[13] He later backed up that assignment with a directive informing the field commanders that "the Reichsführer-SS has been given special tasks . . . resulting from the necessity finally to settle the conflict between two opposing political systems. . . ."[14]

He made the nature of these "special tasks" clear in the infamous Commissars Order of June 6, 1941, ordering the liquidation of all communist officials: "Action must . . . be taken against [the commissars] *immediately*, without further consideration, and with all severity. Therefore, when they are picked up in battle or resistance, they are, as a matter of principle, to be finished immediately with a weapon."[15]

At dawn on June 22, 1941, Germany invaded the Soviet Union with a massive force: 3 million men, three thousand tanks, seven thousand guns (field artillery), and three thousand aircraft.[16] On Himmler's orders, SS units known as *Einsatzgruppen*, "special action groups," followed the regular army into each conquered town or village.

While the army moved on to its next conquest, the Einsatzgruppen went to work. They had one job: to systematically kill Jewish men, women, and children, along with any Soviet commissars the army might have missed. They could wipe out an entire community in a few hours of shooting, filling mass graves with layer upon layer of corpses.

From June 1941 to April 1942, the Einsatzgruppen killed more than seven hundred thousand Jews.[17] Hitler kept his distance from the slaughter. In October 1941, with the Einsatzgruppen killing hundreds of people every day, Hitler remarked that he had found himself "remaining inactive" in regard to the Jews. "There's no sense in adding uselessly to the difficulties of the moment. . . . I tell myself that there's no point in administering pin-pricks, and that for the moment it's preferable to be silent."[18]

By this time, Hitler could afford to be silent on the Jewish question. The mass murder he had authorized and encouraged was taking on a life of its own, with Himmler and Heydrich leading the way. This left Hitler free to concentrate on the war itself.

# 9

# The Road to Ruin

In war, conditions can change with breathtaking speed. From June through November, Hitler seemed to be nothing short of a military genius. Then came December and a series of events that left Germany with a stalled offensive, a new and powerful enemy, and a greatly expanded war. Hitler created some of these problems and made others worse by ignoring his military advisors and generals, planning haphazardly, and not adapting to changing circumstances.

## Reversals of Fortune

On December 5, units of the German Army reached the outskirts of Moscow, only to meet fierce opposition. Hitler expected his commanders to hold their positions, but they could not. All along the front, the Germans fell back, taking heavy casualties.

As they struggled to stabilize their lines, a sudden cold front sent temperatures plunging down to 31° below zero. Weapons became unusable, vehicles stalled in their tracks, and men froze because they did not have proper cold-weather gear. Hitler was so confident of a speedy victory that he considered heavy winter gear unnecessary.

Two days after the debacle on the Eastern Front, Germany's Japanese allies staged a surprise attack on the United States Pacific Fleet at Pearl Harbor, Hawaii. President Franklin D. Roosevelt went on the radio with his famous "day that will live in infamy" speech, and on December 8, the United States declared war on Japan.

The German General Staff held its collective breath, fearing that Roosevelt would declare war on Germany as well. The Führer had given standing orders not to antagonize the Americans; he wanted to keep them out of the war at all costs. No one was prepared for his sudden change of heart. On December 11, without advance warning to anyone, Hitler declared war on the United States.

Historian Martin Gilbert called this "perhaps the greatest error, and certainly the single most decisive act, of the Second World War."[1] Germany was already outmanned and out-gunned; with the United States entering the war, the odds against Germany became overwhelming.

## Hitler and the "Final Solution to the Jewish Question"

Overwhelming odds or not, Adolf Hitler meant to fight one more enemy: the Jews. Since *Mein Kampf*, he had been saying in one way or another that the next war would destroy the Jews. In 1931, he said that if war broke out, the Jews would be "crushed by the wheels of history."[2] In 1935, "If a foreign army, under orders of the Jews, should ever enter

German territory then it will have to march over the corpses of slain Hebrews."[3]

In 1939, there was the infamous "prophesy" in a speech to the Reichstag: "If the international Jewish financiers in and outside Europe should succeed in plunging the nations once more into a world war, then the result will not be the Bolshevization of the earth, and thus the victory of Jewry, but the annihilation of the Jewish race in Europe."[4]

Hitler's threats told what he wanted to do, but not how he intended to do it. By order of Hermann Göring, official coordinator of Nazi Jewish policy, the job of creating a comprehensive plan for the "final solution to the Jewish question" fell to Reinhard Heydrich.

On January 20, 1942, Heydrich summoned fifteen leading Nazis to a secret meeting on the shores of Berlin's Wannsee Lake. Heydrich's job was to involve high-ranking bureaucrats in organizing and implementing the program. The killing itself had already begun. The first death camp, Chelmno, was already in operation and others were being constructed.

The Wannsee Protocols established rules and procedures for mass killing on a scale that had never been seen before. Men, women, and children were packed into boxcars and shipped to killing centers, equipped with gas chambers and massive crematory ovens. Upon arrival, most of every "shipment" went straight from the train to the gas chambers.

## Operation Blue

When the Final Solution got under way, Hitler left administration to underlings and turned his attention to the Eastern Front, with a summer offensive to begin in June 1942. Its objectives were to conquer the city of Stalingrad and take over the oil fields in the Caucasus.

Field Marshal Fedor von Bock opened the offensive by capturing the city of Voronezh. He was supposed to wrap it up quickly, then head south to reinforce troops trying to keep an enemy force surrounded and unable to move. Instead, Bock got tied up with a Russian counterattack. This delayed his arrival in the south by two days and allowed enemy troops to escape capture. Hitler raged at Bock, then fired him. This was the first of many confrontations between the Führer and his generals during Operation Blue.

The conflicts usually centered around Hitler's command style. He issued impulsive and confusing orders, ignored expert strategists, and based important military decisions on his own "intuition."

In July 1942, with little forethought or preparation, Hitler decided to change tactics. Instead of first conquering Stalingrad, then moving on to the Caucasian oil fields, he decided to split his forces and attack both targets at the same time. He had convinced himself that the Soviets did not have the resources to stop this new German offensive.

Over the objections of his generals, Hitler gave the order that divided German forces, sending a large force to the Caucasus region and a smaller one to Stalingrad. Chief of the General Staff Franz Halder saw a disaster in the making, yet could do nothing to stop it.

In his diary, Franz Halder wrote that

> [Hitler's] chronic tendency to underrate enemy capabilities is gradually assuming grotesque proportions and develops into a positive danger. The situation is getting more and more intolerable. There is no room for any serious work. This so-called leadership is characterized by a pathological reacting to the impressions of the moment and a total lack of any understanding of the command machinery and its possibilities.[5]

## The Battle for Stalingrad

Largely because of Hitler's misjudgments, the summer offensive did not reach its objectives. In the Caucasus Mountains, the Germans captured the Maykop oil field, only to discover that the retreating Soviets had systematically destroyed the wells.

At Stalingrad, the German Sixth Army under General Friedrich Paulus had penetrated deep into the city before the Soviets drove them back with an overwhelming offensive. By November 23, the Sixth Army was encircled and about to be overrun. Paulus asked Hitler for permission to surrender, only to be told that he should fight "to the last soldier and the last bullet."[6]

General Paulus held out for another nine days before finally surrendering on January 31, 1943. By that time, the siege of Stalingrad had cost at least 100,000 German lives, with another 113,000 men taken captive. Only a few thousand of these prisoners of war would survive their time in Russian hands.[7]

In the aftermath of this military disaster, Hitler blamed Paulus, the other field commanders, even the general staff in Berlin, anything and anyone other than himself. This time, the familiar dodge did not spare him from widespread criticism.

Former ambassador to Rome Ulrich von Hassell summarized public reaction in a diary entry for February 14, 1943:

> For the first time Hitler was not able to get out from under the responsibility; for the first time the critical rumours are aimed straight at him. There has been exposed for all eyes to see the lack of military ability of "the most brilliant strategist of all time," that is, our megalomaniac corporal. This was concealed up to now by a few intuitive master strokes, the lucky results of risks that were in themselves unjustified, and the shortcomings of our enemies. It is clear to all that

precious blood has been shed foolishly or even criminally for purposes of prestige alone. Since strictly military affairs are involved this time, the eyes of the generals were opened, too.[8]

In the aftermath of Stalingrad, Hitler became something of a recluse. He stopped going out among the people, rarely gave speeches, and spent little time in Berlin. A leader who owed his power to a cult of personality could not afford this kind of isolation. The more "invisible" he became, the more criticism he received as the war turned steadily against Germany.

## A Dangerous Man

The Eastern Front never recovered from Stalingrad. In the first months of 1944, it collapsed altogether. The Soviets advanced with a crushing attack, retaking much of the territory that had been lost the year before.

In the midst of this pitched battle, Hitler diverted his attention to the Final Solution. He had long been disturbed by the fact that Hungary, one of his allies, was sheltering an intact community of 750,000 Jews. Hungarian leader Miklós Horthy had so far refused to surrender them to the Reich.

Now, Hitler was tired of waiting. With ruthless speed, he sent an occupying force into Hungary, then simply replaced Horthy's government with one that would cooperate. Between May 15 and July 8, 1944, 147 trains carried 437,402 Hungarian Jews to the gas chambers at Auschwitz-Birkenau in Poland.[9]

While Germany killed Jews in Hungary and fought a losing battle on the Eastern Front, the United States and Great Britain launched the biggest amphibious invasion in history. On June 6, 1944, which would forever after be remembered as D-Day, Allied troops landed on the beaches of Normandy, in

France. They would close from the west while the Soviets forced Germany to retreat in the east.

Still, Hitler refused to allow retreat. By his order, thousands of German soldiers fought to the death in a hopeless war. German civilians died in almost-continuous Allied bombing raids; the Luftwaffe could offer little more than token resistance. At a time when many Germans worried about being charged with war crimes in connection with the Final Solution, Hitler wanted to keep killing Jews as long as possible. He made it clear that the death and the fighting would continue so long as he was alive.

A group of Wehrmacht officers had been trying to assassinate Hitler, but they could not get anyone close enough to act. Then in June 1944, Colonel Claus von Stauffenberg was promoted to a position that gave him direct access to Hitler's briefings. On July 20, Von Stauffenberg came to the meeting with a time bomb in his briefcase. He set it on the floor near Hitler, then was summoned to answer a prearranged telephone call.

Moments after Von Stauffenberg left the room, the bomb exploded, with a blast so powerful it blew out the windows and filled the room with thick, black smoke. Some victims lay motionless in the rubble. Others stumbled through the smoke, trying to make their way out of the room. Four of the victims would later die of their injuries.

By a fluke, Hitler was not one of them. He had been partly sheltered by the thick leg of the conference table. The explosion burst his eardrums and shredded his clothes; otherwise, he had only superficial cuts and burns.

**A stunned Hitler views the devastation left by an Allied bombing raid.**

Von Stauffenberg and three others were captured and executed immediately. SS investigations revealed that the conspiracy had involved dozens of people, including several high-ranking officers of the Wehrmacht. For Adolf Hitler, it was a sobering discovery. He began to see traitors everywhere: "Now I know why all my great plans in Russia had to fail in recent years," he told Albert Speer. "It was all treason! But for those traitors, we would have won long ago. Here is my justification before history."[10]

According to Speer, in an "outburst of murderous rage against the conspirators," Hitler vowed to "'annihilate and exterminate' every one of them."[11]

Having figured out "the truth" and purged the traitors, a newly optimistic Hitler believed he could change the course of the war. Other Nazi leaders knew it was far too late to salvage the situation, but none of them would mention that in his presence. They had long since learned to tell him only what he wanted to hear.

## Hitler's Bunker

January 16, 1945, was a critical day in Berlin; it was the day Hitler and his inner circle moved below ground to escape the constant bombing that was turning Berlin into smoldering ruins. Architect Albert Speer described the bunker as "nothing but a great windowless block of concrete" with walls sixteen and a half feet thick. The whole structure was buried fifty-five feet below ground. To Speer, "It seemed as if the concrete walls . . . that surrounded Hitler separated him from the outside world in a figurative as well as literal sense, and locked him up inside his delusions."[12]

Those delusions became the stuff of Hitler's reality. According to writer James P. O'Donnell in his study of Hitler's last days in the bunker, the Führer spent hours planning strategies and troop deployments for armies that no longer existed. At nightly briefings from General Hans Krebs, he

> would give orders for this or that division not to yield an inch, or for this or that city to be defended to the bitter end. But Frankfurt fell, and Kassel, Hanover, and Brunswick. The next night there would be no mention of these cities, just . . . "situational adjustments" on the war map. Hitler was now deploying ghost divisions around Potsdam with the same imperial arrogance with which he had once moved real divisions through France or along the Volga and the Black Sea.[13]

On March 19, he issued a "scorched earth" directive, ordering the destruction of all communications, trucks, trains, bridges, dams, factories, and supplies before the enemy could take them over. When Albert Speer tried to persuade him not to issue the order, Hitler the nationalist, the lover of Germany and all things German, made a chilling reply:

> If the war is to be lost, the nation also will perish. This fate is inevitable. There is no need to consider the basis even of a most primitive existence any longer. On the contrary, it is better to destroy even that, and to destroy it ourselves. The nation has proved itself weak, and the future belongs solely to the stronger eastern nation. Besides, those who remain after the battle are of little value; for the good have fallen.[14]

Speer later expressed shock that Hitler "was deliberately attempting to let the people perish with himself. He no longer knew any moral boundaries; a man to whom the end of his own life meant the end of everything."[15] At this point, Speer decided that he had to defy Hitler's directive. With others of like mind, he worked around-the-clock saving what he could from the Führer's last decree.

**129**

# William L. Shirer

Chicago-born journalist William L. Shirer was working in Germany when Edward R. Murrow of CBS radio offered him a job. Murrow was putting together a new kind of news department, featuring reporters who would see a story through from beginning to end: researching and writing it, then delivering it on the air. Shirer accepted, and became one of the pioneers of broadcast journalism.

He found himself at the right time and place to cover one of the most important events of the twentieth century: the rise of Adolf Hitler and the conflicts that would eventually lead to war.

After being forced out of Germany in 1940, Shirer returned to the United States, where he would later write his National Book Award-winning history of Nazi Germany: *The Rise and Fall of the Third Reich*. Other books followed, including the diaries he kept during those fateful years in Germany.

William L. Shirer eventually settled in Boston, where he died on December 28, 1993, at the age of eighty-nine.

## Gotterdammerung—"Doom of the Gods"

In the bunker, Hitler's inner circle sometimes managed to behave as if life in their concrete dungeon was more or less normal. They ate, they slept, they did routine tasks and talked about routine things. That began to change in mid-April. On the fifteenth, Eva Braun showed up at the bunker unannounced, making it clear that she had come for the duration. A week later, Joseph Goebbels came, with his wife and six children in tow. Through all of this, the deep, booming thunder of Russian artillery sounded constantly in the background.

Late on the night of April 28, Hitler married Eva Braun. The city official who conducted the ceremony dated the marriage certificate "April 28," then noticed that the time was just after midnight. He changed the date to April 29: "Things must be in order," he said.[16]

At a morose "reception," the residents of the bunker toasted the newlyweds with champagne and engaged in determinedly cheerful small talk about the good old days. Then Hitler left his bride in order to dictate his last will and testament to one of his secretaries.

There was nothing new or startling in his last words for posterity. He offered no fresh insights, no apologies, only a litany of hatred that could have come straight from the pages of *Mein Kampf*. His last Führer order brought him full circle, back to the same unreasoning hatred that began his public life: "I charge the leadership of the nation and their followers with the strict observance of the racial laws and with merciless resistance against the universal poisoner of all peoples, international Jewry."[17]

After making his last testament, Hitler began preparing for his death. He wanted to be sure that the poison capsules he

**131**

and Eva Braun planned to take would work. To test them, Hitler ordered his dog trainer to give a capsule to his beloved German shepherd, Blondi. She died instantly. Just after three o'clock in the afternoon, Hitler and his wife bid a formal farewell to those remaining in the bunker and went calmly into his private apartment.

Otto Guensche, one of Hitler's adjutants, waited outside the room to fulfill Hitler's final order: "The last instruction . . . directly from the Fuehrer—was to wait ten minutes and then, and only then, to enter the room. This is just what we did. I kept glancing at my watch. I thought it must have stopped; they were the longest ten minutes of my life."[18]

In the death chamber, Guensche found both Hitler and his new wife dead on the sofa. He had taken poison and also shot himself in the head. She had a small pistol in her hand, but had not used it. According to Hitler's last order, Guensche and his men took the bodies to the chancellery courtyard, doused them in gasoline, and set them afire.

The next day, May 1, 1945, Joseph Goebbels and his wife Magda prepared to follow their Führer in death. In his name, they would not only destroy themselves, but their six young children as well. Magda Goebbels did it herself, poisoning the children as she tucked them into bed. Then she and her husband killed themselves with the poison-and-gunshot method the Führer had used.

So the bunker story ended, with a human sacrifice that shocked even hardened soldiers. All that was left for the survivors was a breakout—a desperate effort to escape the Russian invaders.

In the end, Adolf Hitler did not conquer the world, wipe Russia off the map, or exterminate the Jews. What he did do was transform hatred into a philosophy and death into an industry. He created a world of ghettos, mass execution squads, and killing centers with gas chambers and crematory ovens. At least 11 million people, 6 million of them Jews, died because Adolf Hitler decided they had no right to live. In the process of creating this monstrosity, he became an enduring model of the human capacity for evil—power hungry, self-absorbed, and convinced of his own "superiority."

# A Legacy of Hatred

Comparing Adolf Hitler to other dictators of his time can shed some light on the political, economic, and social realities that shaped a generation of dictators. It can also explore the qualities that set Hitler apart, making this high school dropout into one of the most powerful and ruthless dictators in human history. In the war, Hitler allied himself with or fought against dictators who shared his need for power and would do almost anything to get it: Josef Stalin of the Soviet Union, Benito Mussolini of Italy, and Hideki Tojo of Japan.

## Josef Stalin

Josef Stalin was born Iosif Vissarionovich Dzhugashvili on December 21, 1879. While Hitler came from a financially comfortable middle-class home, Stalin's parents were illiterate peasants, scratching out a living in the Russian state of Georgia. Both were self-made men, but Stalin created his identity as a member of the proletariat, or working class. Hitler wanted to rise above his origins, to achieve great things.

As a communist, Stalin wanted to create a dictatorship of the proletariat and to develop a closely managed economy based on collective ownership of the means of production. His ideal state would be egalitarian, with no class conflict, no rich and no poor, and no private ownership of property.

This was the exact opposite of Hitler's National Socialist ideal. The Nazi ideal did not glorify the working class or call for public ownership of property. It sought to create a natural aristocracy based upon ability rather than wealth, education, or accident of birth.

Both Stalin and Hitler exercised dictatorial powers, both used blood purges to get rid of inconvenient enemies, and both expanded their empires by aggression against smaller, weaker nations. Perhaps the chief difference between them, besides their ideologies, was leadership style. Stalin was a schemer, working behind the scenes to get what he wanted. He lacked Hitler's ability to move the masses.

## Benito Mussolini

Like Hitler and Stalin, Benito Mussolini came from humble circumstances. Born in Romagna, Italy, on July 29, 1883, Mussolini was the son of a blacksmith and a schoolteacher. He bounced from one thing to another in his youth, living on the fringes of society, never quite fitting in anywhere.

Mussolini shared Hitler's abilities as a propagandist and speaker; he instinctively knew how to "work a crowd." Writer George Seldes once described a Mussolini speech in terms reminiscent of Hitler:

> He began coldly, in a voice northern and unimpassioned.
> I had never heard an Italian orator so restrained. Then he
> changed, became soft and warm, added gestures, and

flames in his eyes. The audience moved with him. He held them. Suddenly he lowered his voice to a heavy whisper and the silence among the listeners became more intense. The whisper sank lower and the listeners strained breathlessly to hear. Then Mussolini exploded with thunder and fire, and the mob—for it was no more than a mob now—rose to its feet and shouted. Immediately Mussolini became cold and nordic and restrained again and swept his mob into its seats exhausted.[1]

Mussolini insisted on being in control of everything and everyone. At one time or another, he appointed himself minister of the interior, the colonies, the corporations, the armed services, foreign affairs, and public works, all while serving as prime minister and head of the Fascist party.

Like Hitler and Stalin, Mussolini did not hesitate to purge his enemies. In 1943, he arrested and executed five men who had opposed him in the Fascist Grand Council. One was his son-in-law, Count Galeazzo Ciano. Mussolini could be brutal and even vicious, but he lacked Hitler's deep fascination for death and destruction.

## Hideki Tojo

Hideki Tojo was born on December 30, 1884, in Tokyo, Japan, the son of a general in the Japanese Imperial Army. Unlike Hitler, Tojo did not have to "find himself" through youthful adventures and misadventures. He grew up knowing that bushido, the warrior's code, would shape his life.

He also absorbed his father's fierce nationalism, which included a belief in Japanese racial superiority. Unlike Hitler's "biological" racism, the Japanese view did not pretend to be rooted in science. Its foundation was in mythology, ancient origin tales, in which the Japanese people were descended from the gods.

This could produce anything from snobbery or cruelty to contempt for the lives of people who did not share this divine pedigree. On a personal level, Hideki Tojo was known for being "obstinate, opinionated, intemperate, and combative," even in his youth.[2] As a military man, he was accustomed to giving orders, not working in cooperation with others. This authoritarian style carried over to his career as prime minister and doubtlessly led to political and especially diplomatic blunders.

Tojo was better trained for his job than the largely self-educated Hitler. He also came from a higher stratum of society and was therefore less defensive and more comfortable with his own authority than Hitler. However, this did not make him less brutal to enemies and "inferiors."

After Japan invaded Nanjing, China, in December 1937, Japanese troops slaughtered more than three hundred thousand civilians and prisoners of war. These were not combat-related killings, but outright murders that often involved horrendous tortures. For example, Japanese soldiers disemboweled Chinese civilians, beheaded them, and used them for bayonet practice.

In defeat, Tojo behaved like Hitler, Stalin, and most every other tyrant, blaming his enemies for everything. Tojo claimed that Great Britain and the United States had provoked the war by imposing economic sanctions on Japan, providing aid to China, and preventing Japan from stopping the spread of Soviet-style communism in Asia.[3]

## Adolf Hitler: A Summing Up

Bad as the other World War II dictators might have been, Hitler seems to stand out. He did not force himself on the German people; he won them over with visions of a "national community" and promises of a "master race."

This drawing illustrates German dominance of the Axis alliance, showing Hitler, Benito Mussolini, and Hideki Tojo reading *Mein Kampf* in their respective languages.

However, Hitler was not exceptionally intelligent. Aside from a talent for public speaking, he was simply an ordinary man with poor social skills and a tendency to turn every conversation into a monologue.

In spite of his shortcomings, Hitler reshaped a nation into his own grim image. On his command, people violated their moral principles and went against their better judgment. They launched a war and committed genocide.

However, Hitler's uncanny ability to inspire the masses lasted only so long as Germany appeared to be winning the war. Hitler could not handle the setbacks and disasters that began when the Eastern Front became a nightmare. As the Third Reich came to its end, this man who once captivated people with his words pulled back into himself and had nothing to say at all.

# TIMELINE: The Life of Adolf Hitler

*(Shaded areas indicate events in the life of Adolf Hitler.)*

**1889**

**April 20:** Born to Alois and Klara Hitler.

**1900**

**September 17:** Begins *Realschule*.

**1903**

**January 3:** Father dies.

**1906**

**Spring:** First visit to Vienna.

**1907**

**September:** Fails to pass entrance exam for Academy of Fine Arts.

**December 21:** Mother dies.

**1908**

**October:** Second application to academy is unsuccessful.

**1909–1913**

Homeless in Vienna.

**May 16, 1913:** Receives inheritance from father's estate.

**May 24, 1913:** Leaves Vienna for Munich.

**1914**

**August 16:** Reports for duty in Bavarian Army.

**December:** Receives Iron Cross second class.

**1916**

**October 5:** Wounded in battle.

**1918**

**August 4:** Receives Iron Cross first class.

**October 13–14:** Temporarily blinded in mustard-gas attack.

**October 21:** Transferred to military hospital.

**November 11:** Receives news of Germany's defeat.

**November 21:** Returns to Munich, still in the army.

**1919**

**June 5–12:** Attends political instruction classes.

**August 20:** Begins teaching political instruction classes.

**1919** *(continued)*

**September 13:** Attends first meeting of the German Workers' Party; Later joins.

**September 16:** Assigned to write letter clarifying anti-Semitism.

**1920**

**February 24:** Changes the party name to National Socialist German Workers' Party.

**March 31:** Discharged from the army.

**1921**

**July 11:** Resigns from Nazi party

**July 26:** Rejoins the party, this time as sole leader.

**1922**

**October 8:** Merges Julius Streicher's group into the Nazi party.

**1923**

**November 8–9:** Leads the Beer Hall Putsch.

**1924**

**April 1:** Begins prison term for his role in the putsch.

**December 20:** Paroled from prison.

**1925**

**February:** Begins to reestablish the party.

**July 18:** *Mein Kampf* is published.

**1928**

**August:** Begins relationship with his niece, Geli Raubal.

**1929**

**October:** New York stock market crash.

**1931**

**January 5:** Reappoints Ernst Röhm to head SA.

**September 18:** Geli Raubal commits suicide.

**1932**

**February 22:** Becomes a candidate for president.

**1933**

**January 30:** Becomes chancellor of Germany.

**February 28:** Reichstag fire; Hitler seeks emergency powers.

**March 22:** Concentration camp at Dachau opens.

**April 1:** Calls a one-day boycott of Jewish businesses.

**April 26:** Gestapo established.

**May 10:** Nazis burn banned books in public.

**1934**

**June 30:** Has Ernst Röhm and others executed.

**August 2:** Declares himself chancellor and president after death of Hindenburg.

**1935**

**May 31:** Jews in Germany no longer allowed to serve in armed forces.

**September 13:** Decrees Nuremberg Race Laws.

**1936**

Nazis boycott Jewish-owned businesses.

**March 7:** Sends troops to occupy Rhineland.

**July:** Sachsenhausen concentration camp opens.

**1937**

**July 15:** Buchenwald concentration camp opens.

**1938**

**March:** Mauthausen concentration camp opens.

**1938**  *(continued)*

**March 12:** Annexes Austria to Germany.

**March 13:** Germany annexes Austria and applies all anti-Jewish laws there.

**July 6:** League of Nations holds conference on Jewish refugees at Evian, France, but no action is taken to help the refugees.

**September 29–30:** Signs Munich Pact guaranteeing Czechoslovakian borders.

**October 5:** All Jewish passports must now be stamped with a red "J."

**October 15:** Nazi troops occupy the Sudentenland.

**November 9-10:** Kristallnacht, the Night of the Broken Glass; Jewish businesses and synagogues are destroyed and 30,000 Jews are sent to concentration camps.

**1939**

**January 30:** Claims that Jews will be destroyed if there is a war.

**March:** Takes Czechoslovakia, breaking Munich Pact.

**August 23:** Signs nonaggression pact with the Soviet Union.

**September 1:** Invades Poland; Beginning of World War II.

**1940**

**April 9:** Germans occupy Denmark and southern Norway.

**May 7:** Lodz Ghetto is established.

**May 10:** Germans invade Belgium and the Netherlands.

**May 20:** Auschwitz concentration camp is established.

**June 22:** France surrenders to Germany.

**September 27:** Germany, Italy, and Japan form the Axis powers.

**November 16:** Warsaw Ghetto is established.

## 1941

**February:** Anti-Jewish legislation begins in the Netherlands.

**June 22:** Invades Soviet Union, breaking nonaggression pact.

**October:** Auschwitz II (Birkenau) death camp is established.

**December 11:** Declares war on the United States.

## 1942

British air raids hit Amsterdam.

**January 20:** Wannsee Conference takes place in Berlin where the "Final Solution" is outlined.

**March 17:** Killings begin at Belzec death camp.

**May:** Killings begin at Sobibor death camp.

**July 22:** Treblinka concentration camp is established.

**Summer–Winter:** Mass deportations to death camps begin.

## 1943

**March:** Liquidation of Krakow Ghetto begins.

**April 19:** Warsaw Ghetto uprising.

**Fall:** Liquidation of Minsk, Vilna, and Riga ghettos.

## 1944

**March-May:** Germany occupies Hungary and begins deporting Hungarian Jews.

**July 14:** Soviet forces liberate Majdanek death camp.

**July 20:** Survives an assassination attempt.

**November 8:** Death march of Jews from Budapest to Austria begins.

## 1945

**January 17:** Auschwitz inmates begin death march.

**April 6-10:** Buchenwald inmates sent on death march.

**April 30:** Commits suicide along with his new wife, Eva Braun.

**May 8:** Germany surrenders.

# Chapter Notes

## Chapter 1. A Youth in Austria

1. Hugh Trevor-Roper, *The Last Days of Hitler*, 3rd ed. (London: Macmillan, 1962), p. 46.

2. Robert G. L. Waite, *The Psychopathic God: Adolf Hitler* (New York: Basic Books, 1977), p. 147n.

3. Joachim C. Fest, *Hitler*, trans. Richard and Clara Winston (New York: Harcourt Brace Jovanovich, 1974), p. 14.

4. Waite, p. 155.

5. Adolf Hitler, *Mein Kampf*, trans. Ralph Manheim (Boston: Houghton Mifflin Company, 1971), p. 8. Excerpt from MEIN KAMPF by Adolf Hitler, translated by Ralph Manheim. Copyright © 1943, renewed 1971 by Houghton Mifflin Company. Reprinted by permission of Houghton Mifflin Company. All rights reserved.

6. "Interview with Paula Hitler, 5th June 1946," Modern Military Records (NWCTM), Textural Archives Services Section, National Archives and Records Administration, College Park, Maryland, n.d., <http://www.oradour.info/appcndix/paula01.htm> (February 17, 2004).

7. Franz Zetzinger, *Hitler's Youth* (Westport, Conn.: Greenwood Publishing Group, 1977), pp. 105–106.

8. August Kubizek, *The Young Hitler I Knew* (Boston: Houghton-Mifflin, 1955), pp. 13–14.

9. Ibid., p. 38

10. Hitler, p. 20.

11. Waite, pp. 224–225.

12. Ian Kershaw, *Hitler 1889–1936: Hubris* (New York: W. W. Norton, 1998), p. 63.

13. Hitler, p. 56.

14. Ibid., p. 123.

## Chapter 2. Molding an Identity

1. Adolf Hitler, *Mein Kampf*, trans. Ralph Manheim (Boston: Houghton Mifflin Company, 1971), p. 126. Excerpt from MEIN KAMPF by Adolf Hitler, translated by Ralph Manheim. Copyright © 1943, renewed 1971 by Houghton Mifflin Company. Reprinted by permission of Houghton Mifflin Company. All rights reserved.

2. Ibid., p. 161.

3. Ibid.

4. Norman Cameron and R. H. Stevens, trans., *Hitler's Table Talk 1941–1944: His Private Conversations* (New York: Enigma Books, 2000), p. 44.

5. "Mustard Gas," *Spartacus Educational*, n.p., n.d.,<http://www.spartacus.schoolnet.co.uk/FWWmustard.htm> (March 1, 2004).

6. Hitler, p. 204.

7. "Adolf Hitler's First Antisemitic Writing: September 16, 1919," *H-German Discussion Network*, n.d., <http://www.h-net.msu.edu/~german/gtext/kaiserreich/hitler2.html> (March 3, 2004).

8. Hitler, p. 220.

9. Ibid., p. 223.

10. John Toland, *Adolf Hitler* (New York: Doubleday, 1976), p. 98.

## Chapter 3. Growing Ambitions

1. Adolf Hitler, *Mein Kampf*, trans. Ralph Manheim (Boston: Houghton Mifflin Company, 1971), pp. 548–550. Excerpt from MEIN KAMPF by Adolf Hitler, translated by Ralph Manheim. Copyright © 1943, renewed 1971 by Houghton Mifflin Company. Reprinted by permission of Houghton Mifflin Company. All rights reserved.

2. Ian Kershaw, *Hitler 1889–1936: Hubris* (New York: W. W. Norton, 1998), p. 201.

3. Hitler, p. 679.

4. Kershaw, p. 236.

## Chapter 4. A National Stage

1. Joachim C. Fest, *The Face of the Third Reich: Portraits of the Nazi Leadership* (New York: Pantheon Books, 1970), p. 32.

2. Ibid., p. 31.

3. Joseph Goebbels, *The Early Goebbels Diaries: The Journal of Joseph Goebbels from 1925–1926* (New York: Praeger, 1963), p. 100.

4. Fest, p. 33.

5. Robert G. L. Waite, *The Psychopathic God: Adolf Hitler* (New York: Basic Books, Inc., 1977), p. 259.

6. Ibid., p. 192.

7. Heinrich Hoffmann, *Hitler Was My Friend* (London: Burke, 1955), pp. 157–159.

8. John Toland, *Adolf Hitler* (New York: Doubleday, 1976), p. 256.

9. Ernst Hanfstaengl, *Hitler: The Missing Years* (New York: Arcade Publishing, 1994), pp. 168–169.

10. Nerin Gunn, *Eva Braun* (New York: Bantam Books, 1969), pp. 42–43.

11. Ibid.

12. Ibid.

13. "Nazi party (NSDAP)," *Spartacus Educational*, n.d., <http://www.spartacus.schoolnet.co.uk/GERunemployment.htm> (April 4, 2004).

14. Fest, p. 33.

## Chapter 5. Chancellor Hitler

1. "Weimar Timeline," *MIT OpenCourseWare*, n.d., <http://ocw.mit.edu/NR/rdonlyres/Political-Science/17-508The-Rise-and-Fall-of-Democracy--Regime-ChangeSpring2002/EAAEB706-ED54-4B3B-BFD2-C01B8EC48F6D/0/weimar_timeline.pdf> (December 2, 2004).

2. "Hitler's Speech in Munich: Speech of September 16, 1930," *Humanitas International*, 2001, <http://www.humanitas-international.org/showcase/chronography/speeches/1930-09-16.html> (April 5, 2004).

3. Ibid.

4. Ibid.

5. John Toland, *Adolf Hitler* (New York: Doubleday, 1976), p. 263.

6. Ian Kershaw, *Hitler 1889–1936: Hubris* (New York: W. W. Norton, 1998), p. 368.

7. Ibid., p. 371.

8. "The Triumph of Hitler," *The History Place*, 2001, <http://www.historyplace.com/worldwar2//triumph/tr-army.html> (February 28, 2005).

9. Kershaw, pp. 460, 463.

## Chapter 6. The Making of the Führer

1. Dr. Edgar Feuchtwanger, "Nazi Gleichschaltung," *New Perspective*, vol. 7, no. 2., n.d., <http://www.history-ontheweb.co.uk/concepts/concept72_gleichschaltung.htm> (December 6, 2004).

2. "Hitler's Speech to the Reichstag, Berlin: Speech of March 23, 1933," *Humanitas International*, n.d., <http://www.humanitas-international.org/showcase/chronography/speeches/1933-03-23.html> (December 2, 2004).

3. Ibid.

4. "Hitler's Speech to the Reichstag, Berlin: Speech of March 23, 1933," *Humanitas International*, n.d., <http://www.humanitas-international.org/showcase/chronography/speeches/1933-03-23.html> (December 2, 2004).

5. Dr. Edgar Feuchtwanger, "Nazi Gleichschaltung," *New Perspective*, vol. 7, no. 2., n.d., <http://www.history-ontheweb.co.uk/concepts/concept72_gleichschaltung.htm> (December 6, 2004).

6. Adolf Hitler, *Mein Kampf*, trans. Ralph Manheim (Boston: Houghton Mifflin Company, 1971), p. 183. Excerpt from MEIN KAMPF by Adolf Hitler, translated by Ralph Manheim. Copyright © 1943, renewed 1971 by Houghton Mifflin Company. Reprinted by permission of Houghton Mifflin Company. All rights reserved.

7. "Walter von Reichenau," *Spartacus Educational*, n.d., <http://www.spartacus.schoolnet.co.uk/GERreichenau.htm> (February 10, 2005).

8. "Night of the Long Knives," *Spartacus Educational*, n.d., <http://www.spartacus.schoolnet.co.uk/GERnight.htm> (April 29, 2004).

9. Albert Speer, *Inside the Third Reich* (New York: Galahad Books, 1995), p. 51.

10. "The Fuehrer Oath," *Jewish Virtual Library*, 2004, <http://www.us-israel.org/jsource/Holocaust/oath.html> (April 27, 2004).

11. Frederic T. Birchall, *New York Times*, August 19, 1934, quoted in "Nazi party (NSDAP)," *Spartacus Educational*, n.d.,<http://www.spartacus.schoolnet.co.uk/GERnazi.htm> (April 28, 2004).

12. John Toland, *Adolf Hitler* (New York: Doubleday, 1976), p. 360.

13. Robert G. L. Waite, *The Psychopathic God: Adolf Hitler* (New York: Basic Books, Inc., 1977), pp. 251–252.

14. Ian Kershaw, *Hitler 1889–1936: Hubris* (New York: W. W. Norton, 1998), p. 529.

## Chapter 7. Love, Lebensraum, and Power Struggles

1. Albert Speer, *Inside the Third Reich* (New York: Galahad Books, 1995), p. 91. Reprinted with the permission of Scribner, an imprint of Simon & Schuster Adult Publishing Group, from INSIDE THE THIRD REICH by Albert Speer, translated from German by Richard and Clara Wilson. Copyright © 1969 by Verlag Ulstein GmbH. English Translation Copyright © 1970 by Macmillian Publishing Company.

2. Ibid., p. 92.

3. "The Diary," *Eva Braun: Wife of Adolf Hitler,* n.d., <http://www.shoah.dk/Braun/diary.htm> (April 19, 2004).

4. "Law for the Protection of German Blood and German Honor," *Jewish Virtual Library,* <http://www.us-israel.org/jsource/Holocaust/nurmlaw2.html> (May, 13, 2004).

5. Speer, p. 72.

6. "Hossbach Memorandum," *The Avalon Project: The International Military Tribunal for Germany,* n.d., <http://www.yale.edu/lawweb/avalon/imt/hossbach.htm> (May 12, 2004).

7. Ian Kershaw, *Hitler 1936–1945: Nemesis* (New York: W. W. Norton & Company, 2000), p. 53.

8. Terry Parssinen, *The Oster Conspiracy of 1938* (New York: HarperCollins, 2003), p. 31.

9. "Kurt von Schuschnigg," *Spartacus Educational,* n.d., <http://www.spartacus.schoolnet.co.uk/GERschuschnigg.htm> (May 20, 2004).

10. William L. Shirer, *Berlin Diary* (New York: Galahad Books, 1995), p. 137.

11. Donald M. McKale, *Hitler's Shadow War* (New York: Cooper Square Press, 2002), pp. 97, 99.

12. David Kiley, "End of the road for the 'Love Bug,'" *USA Today,* July 16, 2003, <http://www.usatoday.com/money/autos/2003-07-14-beetle_x.htm> (December 9, 2004).

13. McKale, p. 108.

14. Robert E. Conot, *Justice at Nuremberg* (New York: Harper and Row, 1983), p. 165.

15. "Joseph Goebbels on Kristallnacht," *www.history-of-the-holocaust.org,* n.d., <http://www.history-of-the holocaust.org/LIBARC/ARCHIVE/Chapters/Terror/Kristall/GoebbelK.html> (January 31, 2005).

16. Dr. Harvey R. Kornberg, "Kristallnacht and the Politics of Anti-Semitism in Nazi Germany," Occasional Paper Series, Rider University, <http://www.rider.edu/holctr/papers.html> (December 10, 2004).

17. "Kristallnacht Perspective," *Remember.org,* n.d., <http://www.remember.org/fact.fin.kristal.html> (December 10, 2004).

18. "Marching Toward War: Czechoslovakia," *The March Toward War: The March of Time as Documentary and Propaganda,* n.d., <http://xroads.virginia.edu/~MA04/wood/mot/html/czech.htm> (December 10, 2004).

19. Robert G. L. Waite, *The Psychopathic God: Adolf Hitler* (New York: Basic Books, Inc., 1977), p. 448.

## Chapter 8. The Führer's War

1. Anthony Read and David Fisher, *The Deadly Embrace: Hitler, Stalin, and the Nazi-Soviet Pact 1939–1941* (New York: W. W. Norton and Company, 1988), p. 245.
2. Ibid., p. 285.
3. Ibid.
4. Joachim C. Fest, *Hitler*, trans. Richard and Clara Winston (New York: Harcourt Brace Jovanovich, 1974), p. 47.
5. Albert Speer, *Inside the Third Reich* (New York: Galahad Books, 1995), p. 165. Reprinted with the permission of Scribner, an imprint of Simon & Schuster Adult Publishing Group, from INSIDE THE THIRD REICH by Albert Speer, translated from German by Richard and Clara Wilson. Copyright © 1969 by Verlag Ulstein GmbH. English Translation Copyright © 1970 by Macmillian Publishing Company.
6. Ibid.
7. "Hitler's Plans for Eastern Europe," *Holocaust Awareness: A Time to Bear Witness*, n.d., <http://www.dac.neu.edu/holocaust/Hitlers_Plans.htm> (January 31, 2005).
8. Ibid.
9. Gerhard L. Weinberg, ed., *Hitler's Second Book: The Unpublished Sequel to Mein Kampf by Adolf Hitler* (New York: Enigma Books, 2003), p. 21.
10. Henry Friedlander, *The Origins of Nazi Genocide: From Euthanasia to the Final Solution* (Chapel Hill: University of North Carolina Press, 1995), p. 67.
11. Donald M. McKale, *Hitler's Shadow War* (New York: Cooper Square Press, 2002), p. 192.
12. "Heinrich Himmler," *Jewish Virtual Library*, 2004, <http://www.jewishvirtuallibrary.org/jsource/Holocaust/himmler.html> (September 10, 2004).
13. Peter Padfield, *Himmler* (New York: MJF Books, 1990), p. 323.
14. Ibid., p. 323.
15. "Extract From the Commissar's Order for 'Operation Barbarossa,' June 6, 1941," *Shoah Resource Center*, 2004, <http://www1.yadvashem.org/about_holocaust/documents/part3/doc170.html> (March 4, 2005).

16. "1941: Hitler invades the Soviet Union," *BBC: On This Day,* n.d., <http://news.bbc.co.uk/onthisday/hi/dates/stories/june/22/news id_3526000/3526691.stm> (July 18, 2004).

17. McKale, p. 248.

18. Norman Cameron and R. H. Stevens, trans., *Hitler's Table Talk 1941–1944: His Private Conversations* (New York: Enigma Books, 2000), p. 90.

## Chapter 9. The Road to Ruin

1. James P. Duffy, *Hitler Slept Late and Other Blunders That Cost Him the War* (New York: Praeger Publishers, 1991), p. 103.

2. Mark Roseman, *The Wannsee Conference and the Final Solution* (New York: Metropolitan Books, 2002), p. 26.

3. Ibid.

4. "Extract from the Speech by Hitler, January 30, 1939," *Documents of the Holocaust—Part I,* n.d., <http://www.yadvashem. org/about_holocaust/documents/part1/doc59.html#top> (August 1, 2004).

5. Ian Kershaw, *Hitler 1936–1945: Nemesis* (New York: W. W. Norton & Company, 2000), p. 529.

6. Ibid., p. 549.

7. Ibid., p. 550.

8. Ulrich von Hassell, *The Von Hassell Diaries, 1938–1944: The Story of the Forces Against Hitler Inside Germany, as Recorded by Ambassador Ulrich von Hassell, a Leader of the Movement* (Garden City, N.Y.: Doubleday and Company, 1947), p. 284.

9. Donald M. McKale, *Hitler's Shadow War* (New York: Cooper Square Press, 2002), p. 367.

10. Albert Speer, *Inside the Third Reich* (New York: Galahad Books, 1995), p. 390. Reprinted with the permission of Scribner, an imprint of Simon & Schuster Adult Publishing Group, from INSIDE THE THIRD REICH by Albert Speer, translated from German by Richard and Clara Wilson. Copyright © 1969 by Verlag Ulstein GmbH. English Translation Copyright © 1970 by Macmillian Publishing Company.

11. Ibid., pp. 390–391.

12. Ibid., p. 391.

13. James P. O'Donnell, *The Bunker* (Boston: Houghton Mifflin Company, 1978), pp. 79–80.

14. Alan Bullock, *Hitler: A Study in Tyranny* (New York: Harper & Row, 1962), pp. 774–775.

15. Hugh Redwall Trevor-Roper, *The Last Days of Hitler* (New York: The Macmillan Company, 1947), p. 78.

16. O'Donnell, p. 157.

17. "My Last Political Testament: Adolf Hitler, Berlin, April 29, 1945," *The Holocaust Project*, n.d., <http://www.humanitas-inter national.org/holocaust/htestmnt.htm> (August 5, 2004).

18. O'Donnell, p. 225.

## Chapter 10. A Legacy of Hatred

1. George Seldes, *You Can't Print That! The Truth Behind the News 1918–1928* (New York: Payson & Clarke Ltd., 1929), p. 105.

2. Mostafa Rejai and Kay Phillips, *World Military Leaders: A Collective and Comparative Analysis* (Westport, Conn.: Praeger Publishers, 1996), p. 103.

3. Ibid., p. 104.

# Glossary

*(Italicized words are German.)*

***Anschluss***—Literally, annexation; the German takeover of Austria.

**Antisemitism**—Hatred of Jews as a people.

**Aryanization**—A code word for the German takeover of Jewish property.

**bunker**—An underground shelter.

**chancellor**—Head of state in a parliamentary government.

**civil commissar**—A government official in the Soviet Union.

**concentration camp**—A prison for political enemies of the ruling regime.

**crematory**—Special ovens for burning human remains.

***Einsatzgruppen***—SS "killing squads" that followed the German army into Russia.

**euthanasia**—Literally, "good death;" Nazi plan to kill the disabled and mentally ill.

**evolution**—Theory that life developed from simpler to more complex forms; "survival of the fittest."

**Final Solution**—A Nazi plan to kill all the Jews of Europe.

***Führer* myth**—Faith in the personal power of Adolf Hitler.

***Führer* oath**—The soldier's oath to the person of Adolf Hitler rather than the German nation.

**ghetto**—A rundown neighborhood set aside for Jewish habitation.

***Gleichschaltung***—The process by which the Nazi Party took over German society.

**League of Nations**—International organization; precursor to the United Nations.

***Lebensraum***—Literally, "living space;" the notion that Germany must expand its territory in order to survive as a nation.

**Life Unworthy of Life**—People considered "defective" by the Nazi regime.

**mustard gas**—A poison gas that was used in World War I.

**Nuremberg Laws**—Hitler's first major antisemitic laws.

**Night of the Long Knives**—The political killing of Ernst Röhm and others considered to be traitors to Adolf Hitler.

**Operation Barbarossa**—Code word for the German invasion of the Soviet Union.

**paramilitary**—A private force that is organized like an army.

**plebiscite**—A direct vote of the electorate rather than an action by a governing body.

**propaganda**—Systematic promotion of a particular cause or doctrine.

**purge**—In politics, the systematic elimination of troublesome people within a regime.

**Putsch**—A revolution from within.

**racism**—The belief that one's own racial group is superior to others.

**Socialism**—A system of government in which the means of production is collectively owned.

**synagogue**—A Jewish House of Worship.

**tuberculosis**—A "wasting disease" that attacks the lungs.

**virulent**—Infectious or malignant; poisonous.

**Volkisch**—German folkways; the culture that binds Germans to one another.

**Wannsee Protocols**—The Nazi plan for implementing the Final Solution.

**Wehrmacht**—The combined armed forces of wartime Germany.

# Further Reading

## Books on Adolf Hitler

Damon, Duane. *Mein Kampf: Hitler's Blueprint for Aryan Supremacy.* San Diego: Lucent Books, 2003.

Fuchs, Thomas. *A Concise Biography of Adolf Hitler.* New York: Berkeley Publishing Group, 2000.

Giblin, James Cross. *The Life and Death of Adolf Hitler.* New York: Clarion Books, 2002.

Hanfstaengl, Ernst. *Hitler: The Missing Years.* New York: Arcade Publishing Co., 1994.

Harris, Nathaniel. *The Rise of Hitler.* Chicago: The Heinemann Library, 2004.

Kershaw Ian, Gerhard Wilke, and Detley Peukert. *The "Hitler Myth:" Image and Reality in the Third Reich.* New York: Oxford University Press, 2001.

Shirer, William L. *The Rise and Fall of Hitler.* New York: Random House Books for Young Readers, 1963.

## Books on the Holocaust

Bauer, Yehuda. *The History of the Holocaust.* With the assistance of Nili Keren. New York: Franklin Watts, 2001.

Boas, Jacob. *We Are Witnesses: Five Diaries of Teenagers Who Died in the Holocaust.* New York: Scholastic, 1996.

Greenfield, Howard. *After the Holocaust.* New York: Greenwillow Books, 2001.

Jaegermann, Judith. *My Childhood in the Holocaust.* Jerusalem, Mazo Publishers, 2004.

Russo, Marisabina. *Always Remember Me: How One Family Survived World War II.* New York: Atheneum Books for Young Readers, 2005.

Shuter, Jane. *Prelude to the Holocaust.* Chicago: Heinemann Library, 2003.

——. *Daily Life in the Camps.* Oxford: Heinemann Library, 2003.

## Books on Nazi Germany

Evans, Richard J. *The Coming of the Third Reich.* New York: Penguin Books, 2004.

## Books on Nazi Germany *(continued)*

Gilbert, G. M. *Nuremberg Diary.* New York: Da Capo Press, 1995.

Shirer, William L. *Berlin Diary: The Journal of a Foreign Correspondent, 1934–1941.* Maryland: Johns Hopkins University Press, 2002.

Speer, Albert. *Inside the Third Reich.* New York: Simon and Schuster, 1997.

Steinhoff Johannes, Peter Pechel, and Dennis Showalter. *Voices From the Third Reich: An Oral History.* New York: Da Capo Press, 1994.

Woodstrom, Annelee. *War Child: Growing Up in Adolf Hitler's Germany.* Self-published, 2003.

## Books on Hitler's Associates

Fest, Joachim C. *The Face of the Third Reich.* New York: Da Capo Press, 1999.

Junge, Trudi. *Until the Final Hour: Hitler's Last Secretary.* New York: Arcade Publishing, 2004.

Nesbit, Roy Convers, and George Van Acker. *The Flight of Rudolf Hess: Myths and Reality.* London: Sutton Publishing, 2003.

Neville, Peter. *Mussolini.* London: Routledge, 2004.

Padfield, Peter. Himmler: *A Full-Scale Biography of One of Hitler's Most Ruthless Executioners.* New York: MJF Books, 1990.

Read, Anthony. *The Devil's Disciples: Hitler's Inner Circle.* New York: W. W. Norton and Company, 2004.

## Books on World War II

Armitage, Michael, John Stanier, Terry Charman, Peter Kornicki, John Pimlott, and G. T. Tiederman. *World War II Day by Day.* New York: D.K. Publishing, Inc., 2004.

Davidson, Edward, and Dale Manning. *Chronology of World War Two.* New York: Sterling Publishing, 1999.

Gilbert, Martin. *The Second World War: A Complete History.* New York: Owl Books, 2004.

Keegan, John. *The Second World War.* New York: Penguin Books, 1990.

Ross, Stewart. *The Blitz: At Home in World War Two.* London: Evans Brothers Ltd., 2001.

*World War II: Day by Day.* New York: DK, 2004.

## Internet Addresses

**BBC Historic Figures: Adolf Hitler.**
<http://www.bbc.co.uk/>

> *Click on "History" at the left. Click on "Historic Figures." Click on "H." Select "Adolf Hitler."*

**Jewish Virtual Library. "Adolf Hitler."**
<http://www.jewishvirtuallibrary.org/>

> *Click on "Enter the Library." Select "Biography." Click on "H." Scroll down and select "Adolf Hitler."*

**The *Time* 100: Leaders and Revolutionaries. Adolf Hitler.**
<http://www.time.com/>

> *Click on "Special Reports" at left. Under "Nation," select "Time 100." In lower right corner, click on "The 1999 Time 100." Under "Leaders and Revolutionaries," click on "Hitler."*

## Video/DVD

*Air War Europe WWII—Liberation of Europe (1998)*, Superior Promotions, Inc.

*Hitler, A Career*, Christian Herrendoerfer and Joachim C. Fest.

*Holocaust & Yad Vashem*, Parade Studio.

*Last Days of WWII*, A&E Entertainment.

# Index